According to what Jesus taught, discipt
tasks of the church. As followers of (y
challenging contexts brought about by   i-
religious cultures, discipling believer   his
book, *Called to Discipleship*, Dănuț Jemna introduce_   nic
perspective of discipleship for changing times. The need for authentic relations
and for building communities that contribute to the transformation of their
members calls for fresh and creative ways to pursue Jesus's call to discipleship.

Otniel Bunaciu, PhD
Professor of Historical Theology,
Dean of Facultatea de Teologie Baptista,
Universitatea din Bucuresti, Romania

The costly art of discipleship – as a commitment and a way of life, not a meth-
odology or a programme – has become rare in our Christian communities.
Dănuț Jemna's book invites us to take a fresh look at the way Jesus went about
making disciples as an inspiration for rediscovering this vital practice for the
followers of Christ in the twenty-first century.

Dănuț Mănăstireanu, PhD
Research Associate,
Institute for Orthodox Research Studies,
University of Cambridge, UK

The verb *mathēteuō* (to make disciples) from the great post-Paschal commandment of Jesus (Matt 28:19) is an imperative not to reflect on discipleship, as
a state that defines Christian identity, but to go out into the world and make
disciples of Jesus. This book, by what it tells us is a step, mine and yours, towards the world where people await us as missionaries. That's why after you
read it, it doesn't close! It always remains open for you to see where you are in
the "work of discipleship." So don't close it!

Stelian Tofană, PhD
Professor of New Testament,
Faculty of Orthodox Theology,
Universitatea din Bucuresti, Romania

Called to Discipleship

GLOBAL LIBRARY

Called to Discipleship

Reflections on the Gospel of Mark

Dănuț Jemna

© 2023 Dănuț Jemna

Published 2023 by Langham Global Library
An imprint of Langham Publishing
www.langhampublishing.org

Langham Publishing and its imprints are a ministry of Langham Partnership

Langham Partnership
PO Box 296, Carlisle, Cumbria, CA3 9WZ, UK
www.langham.org

ISBNs:
978-1-83973-861-6 Print
978-1-83973-886-9 ePub
978-1-83973-887-6 PDF

British Library Cataloguing-in-Publication Data
A catalogue record for this book is available from the British Library

ISBN: 978-1-83973-861-6

Cover & Book Design: projectluz.com

Interior Images: © Ciprian-Ionatan Cotleț

To my wife,
Ligia

Contents

Preface to the Romanian Edition

This book was born out of a particular context, determined by several factors. I would like to mention two of them. The first is the training of young people, in which I have been involved in various forms over the years. Besides the meetings, book readings and debates, these young people also requested tools for their personal development. At several seminars on formation held over the last two years, the need for a text on the basics of Christian discipleship as practiced and passed on by Jesus Christ to his disciples has crystallized.

Another factor is my own writing discipline. After retiring from clerical ministry in 2018, I decided to invest more energy in writing on Christian theology and spirituality. Some of these pieces have been published on my personal blog (https://danutj.wordpress.com), and others have been published as articles or have become chapters for books I am working on. Initially, I wanted to produce a tool for guided reading of the Gospel of Mark, which provided an opportunity to make some observations on the theme of discipleship. This is how the texts on this topic were born. Some chapters were first published on the blog. Subsequently, I have made some improvements and I have added a few more sections. That is how the present book came about.

I would like to thank a few people who participated in one way or another in the publication of the book. First of all, I am grateful to my Lord and master Jesus Christ for yet another opportunity to be close to him on his journey in the world, for support and inspiration in understanding things concerning his work of discipleship. I also thank Ciprian-Ionatan Cotleţ for his openness in creating a series of graphic elements that visually preface the theme of each chapter. I have to mention also the members of the Christian Reading and Dialogue Group of Iași, a dynamic group I have been coordinating for more than 20 years, for their willingness to read the manuscript of this book together and to evaluate the way in which it meets the needs of today's reader. They contributed suggestions during the reading and also offered some thoughts for readers that appear in the afterword. I would like to underline Mihaela David's effort in reading the whole book and suggesting corrections to the text. Further, I remember my friend Dănuţ Mănăstireanu, who kindly wrote the Foreword to this book and always encouraged me to complete this project, being convinced of the need for contextual reflections on this subject. Last but not least, I would like to mention the staff of Casa Cărţii Publishing House, who were involved in the whole process from the reception of the manuscript to the appearance of this book in bookstores.

Dănuţ Jemna

Iaşi, 2019

Preface to the English Edition

The English translation and publication of this book requires two more brief comments in addition to those presented in the preface to the Romanian edition.

The first concerns the fact that, in the English version, the editors suggested adding a set of questions at the end of each chapter, which could serve as a study guide for readers. I have followed this very good idea and added some questions that invite readers to analyse the theme of discipleship in their own lives and in the context of the community and socio-cultural space in which they live. I hope this guide can be useful to reading or Bible study groups interested in the Gospel of Mark and the theme of discipleship.

The second comment relates to the fact that in this book the reader will not find references to the literature, as is usually the case when considering a topic that has been studied by other authors. The explanation for this approach is somehow implicit in the preface of the Romanian edition. This book was born as an evaluative effort and is therefore neither a biblical commentary nor a monograph on discipleship. I read the Gospel of Mark to examine my own experience of understanding and applying discipleship in both my personal life and pastoral ministry. However, this reflection involved not only my own experience, but also reading important books over 20 years of ministry. Some of these are presented in the references section at the end.

In closing, I would like to thank Langham Publishing for their decision to publish this book so that it may reach a wider number of Christians and ministers interested in Christian discipleship. I would also like to thank my friend Dănuț Mănăstireanu for the effort to read and edit the English version of the book.

Dănuț Jemna
Iaşi, 2023

Foreword

*T*he *Times They Are a-Changin'* is the title of one of Bob Dylan's best-known songs, which was written in 1964. Four years later, the youth uprising that was to change the Western world in a fundamental way broke out. Leftism (a mortal sin for the ideologies of the "Christian right"), rebellion against the system, violence, but also flower-power pacifism, drug abuse (including powerful hallucinogens), excessive or deviant sexuality, nonconformist appearance (jeans, boys with long hair) and the other things that characterized this movement scared the ecclesiastical establishment. The young people who met Christ in the wake of this movement (the so-called "Jesus people") were most often rejected, like a foreign body, by traditional churches.

Where Was the Church When the Youth Exploded?, wondered pastor Stuart Briscoe a few years later, in a book unjustly forgotten that carried the same title. Each of these excesses, Briscoe argued, was a cry of despair, but the church in its typical conformism was frightened off by the spectre of change. (As in a well-known joke: to the question, "How many Christians does it take to change a light bulb?" the church's answer would have been: "Change?") The church, then, remained deaf to the calls of the young. Thus, out of necessity, Calvary Chapel emerged as a space to ecclesially accommodate these strange seekers of salvation.

The above are just snatches of somewhat recent stories, but they have been repeated countless times throughout history, before and after the traumatic events of 1968. We too are living in "new times." The fall of communism, but also the excesses of neoliberal capitalism; the dominance of postmodernity – with its legitimate challenge to the dominant narrative promoted by the rationalism of modernity, but also with the derangements of the relativism with which it has set out to replace it; climate change and the profound ecological crisis into which the world has been plunged, because of a perverted (or non-existent) theology of creation, but above all because of the limitless pursuit of profit, at the cost of self-destruction; rampant secularization, in response to the perverse matrimony of ecclesial power with political power, and desecularization, a phenomenon which often leads to the search for spirituality in the absence of transcendence, or worse, to fundamentalist religious fanaticism; as well as the terrible challenges brought about by transhumanism and the irresponsible use of the possibilities offered by modern genetics – these and many others like them have brought our world to the brink of an unprecedented crisis.

This being the case, it is legitimate to ask what is the church doing in the face of all these challenges, apart from living with nostalgia for a supposedly glorious past or desperately trying to restore a Christendom in which it could dictate the rules of the game and which, thank God, has disappeared once and for all. We also wonder how theology responds to this crisis, apart from the theoretical, sterile, and often irrelevant speculations from the perspective of the world we live in – pitiful storms in a glass of water – in which it has been indulging for some time. While in the glorious patristic or medieval ages, if not in the Renaissance and Reformation also, theology was regarded as a veritable queen of humanities, it has nowadays lost its credibility and prestige.

Miroslav Volf and Matthew Croasmun attempt to respond to this disappointing state of affairs in their recent manifesto titled *For the Life of the World: Theology That Makes a Difference*. Thus, Christian theology, from its beginnings, has been rooted in the metaphor of the incarnation. In its best and most authentic manifestations, theology has sought to respond, from the perspective of revelation, understood in the context of history, to the challenges of the world in every age. From this perspective, it is legitimate to ask what a Christian theology engaged in an authentic and unillusioned – that is, realistic and humble – dialogue with the present reality, should look like. I will try, briefly, to list here what I consider to be the essential features of such an approach, so that it can "make a difference" (as the contemporary cliché goes), so that it can have an impact, not as to impose on the world some predetermined solutions, according to some religious textbook standards, but in order to find, together with all those concerned, the way towards the flourishing of human beings and of society in general.

First and foremost, such a theology should focus not so much on formulating sophisticated speculative elaborations, but on creating viable and transmittable models of engagement with reality, both at the personal and community level. This does not mean to abandon conceptual rigour and the value of rationality – undeniable gains of modernity – but to use them not as ends in themselves but as tools for achieving human flourishing.

Second, to be transformative, theology should abandon the individualistic, autarchic approach dominant in the Enlightenment, for a communitarian one. This means, first of all, that it needs to return, with weapons and baggage, to the ecclesial space as a constitutive and hermeneutically validating instance. This, however, is only the first step; to limit it to this would be to stop halfway. The second absolutely necessary step is to root this effort in the extra-ecclesial worldly space, which gives theology a holistic, if not cosmic dimension (according to the principle enunciated by the apostle Paul in Eph 1:10).

In such a context, science becomes an unavoidable dialogue partner for theology, to the benefit of both disciplines. Science would thus receive from theology essential questions about the purpose and legitimacy of its endeavours, while theology would be challenged to consider new aspects of reality as revealed by science, thus constantly verifying and adjusting its conclusions in order to continue being, for those who have ears to hear, a trustworthy guide for the advancement of life.

One of the most formidable challenges that science brings to the Christian theologian is in the area of anthropology – a theological discipline largely neglected in the twenty centuries of Christian thought. It is quite possible that, just as ecclesiology was the central theological focus of the twentieth century, anthropology will play a key role in the theological debates of the present century. Here I am referring not only to the questions raised by the emergence of the transhumanist phenomenon, human-machine interaction, or the risks inherent in genetic manipulation that no longer take into account the ethical rigours agreed by the scientific community, but also to the need for a more nuanced understanding of transsexuality, gender relations, the family, or the patriarchalism and misogyny that still dominate most societies, including the most developed ones.

Postmodernity brings with it another challenge to Christian theology, in terms of defining the concept of authority, by shifting the emphasis from *dunamis* – authority as power, as an imposing instance, to *exousia* – authority as a building, growing and maturing instance. After the excesses of authority – ecclesial, but not only – in the medieval period, and the radical contestation of authority seen as intrinsically oppressive in modernity and, differently nuanced, in postmodernity, Christian theology is called to embody a rather humble, "bottom-up," serving and constituting understanding of authority; not one that imposes itself by virtue of its institutional and positional prerogatives, but one that is seductive and seminal.

Institutions have conceptually and structurally dominated the modern world. Despite their undoubted added value – in transcending the inherent limitations of structures built around individuals, whether part of an aristocracy or endowed with a particular charisma or vision – institutions seem to have reached the limits of their potential, leaving more and more room today for networking approaches – admittedly more fluid, but also more flexible and capable to adapt more promptly to the rapid changes in the world we live in.

Another challenge facing contemporary theology has to do with the nature of Scripture and with the hermeneutical process by which believers can understand God's expectations of how they are called upon to represent him in the world. The textbook approaches inherited from fundamentalism (which is nothing more than the literalist face of the coin of rationalist liberalism – in which believers approach the sacred text with their questions in order to receive supposedly unique "biblical answers" that transcend time, culture, and context) have already proven their irrational and often aberrant character. Postmodernity proposes that we rediscover revelation (whether we speak of what is formally inscribed in the canon of Scripture or of the living tradition of the Spirit's presence throughout the centuries in the ecclesial community and in the world) as an invitation to an initiation journey, or as an "entry into the story," like that of the hero Atreyu in the movie *Neverending Story*. In this new adventure of faith, Scripture is not a map but rather a compass, the obvious implication being that theology finds its legitimacy only through an ongoing dialogue with God and the world.

Most of Christian history has been dominated by the understanding of theology as an approach addressed (predominantly, if not exclusively) to the religious person. The secularism that now dominates many developed societies, especially in the West, and the post-secular phenomenon that is increasingly present around us, bring forward a reality that was until recently a marginal one. If we have an eye for it, we will see around us more and more people who, for various reasons, are disillusioned with the church or with religion in general, even with God (as presented to us by religious institutions), but who continue to be in search of spirituality, defined in various ways. Sometimes such people declare themselves to be atheists, agnostics, or just sceptics, and not infrequently talk about themselves as being "spiritual but not religious." Such ambiguities often paralyse and agitate Christians, who, instead of identifying the opportunity for the renewal of their own faith that interaction with this group represents, become defensive or apologetic, instinctively resorting to the aggressive toolkit of proclamation and predominantly conceptual persuasion, which is thought to have borne some fruit in the modern period, but which is totally inadequate in the case of postmodern person. This contemporary phenomenon calls us to reimagine Christian witness as an apologetic of love, as good news for the non-religious person, who is not called to conform to a dominant ideology or to join a constraining institution, but to join other seekers in this new yet perennial adventure of faith.

You may wonder how the above considerations relate to the book on discipleship in Mark's Gospel that this text attempts to preface. For my part, I prefer to let you discover for yourselves the answer to that question, assuming there is one, and I would rather tell you why I think this book was necessary and, more importantly, why it would be worth reading.

The idea of apprenticeship/discipleship, as a training method, is by no means a new one. It predates the coming of Jesus into the world, being present in both Greek and Jewish culture, not only in philosophical or religious training, but also in professional formation, the main sense in which it has continued to exist to this day. Apprenticeship was the main mode of transmission of Christian thought and life during the first three centuries of the church. After Constantine, however, when the citizens of the empire became Christians by decree, discipleship fell into disuse and continued to be practised as such almost exclusively in monastic circles.

Even now, seventeen centuries later, the situation is not much better. Apprenticeship, mainly as a method and training programme rather than as a way of life, experienced a revival in the middle of the last century and reached us in Romania in the late seventies through Western Christian organisations such as the Navigators. Very quickly, however, after less than ten years, the old idea of training under the guidance of a master, rediscovered by evangelicals, was transformed in our country, under the pressure of American pragmatism, into a kind of apprenticeship franchise, the unfortunate result being the multiplication of programmes and discipleship groups concerned with studying the same material together (such as *Discipleship in the School of Jesus* – the so-called Colossians 2:7 series, or the question-and-answer study guides produced by Navigators or Campus Crusade). Thus, through the use of unfortunate methodological approaches, similar to serial production, which is incompatible with the Christian ethos and tradition, Christian discipleship was soon "buried" in the Romanian evangelical environment, despite the best intentions of the initiators. Today, only a few nostalgic people continue to talk about discipleship, and the number of those who still really practise it is even smaller. As a result, those who feel attracted by it have no idea what it really is or where they could find a master willing to pay the price for their training.

It cannot be said that those interested in this subject do not have at their disposal useful materials in the Romanian language. In addition to Robert Coleman's excellent book, *The Master's Plan of Evangelism* (in fact, despite the title, a book about the discipleship model practiced by Jesus), Walt Henrichsen's book *Disciples Are Made, not Born*, and the course on *Evangelism and Discipleship* (significantly renamed *Evangelism and Faith Building*) published before 1989 by BEE, Romanians now have at their disposal Juan Carlos Ortiz's exceptional book on discipleship, published by Casa Cărţii. Nevertheless, to my knowledge, there has not been published yet a significant text on this subject that is written by a Romanian evangelical Protestant. Dănuț Jemna's book is a first.

Theology, in the true sense of the word, is a spiritual and intellectual approach which is contextualized in time and space and is firmly rooted in the data of revelation. For those interested in discipleship as worked out in the concreteness of the Romanian cultural context, it is not enough to understand how this discipline is practiced by American Christians or how it manifests itself in monastic settings. That is why a book on discipleship whose Romanian author has a solid biblical and theological grounding is extremely important, if not absolutely necessary for such an approach. Especially so, since the author's expertise on this subject is not limited to the theological domain – these skills are complemented in his case by almost three decades of practice in discipleship and mentoring, both in terms of Christian formation and professional training, which increases the overall value of his book.

Dănuț Jemna is not only a genuine spiritual teacher, as evidenced by the number of those who regard him as an authority in their walk with Christ, but also a ministry partner with whom, despite our obvious differences, I have had the privilege of being associated over the past decades, to the benefit of both of us. That is why I warmly recommend this book, as one who has witnessed the entire process, from its birth to the present form.

Called to Discipleship, like any authentic theological endeavour, is a call to a new spiritual pilgrimage. If you will use it merely to furnish your mind, the author's efforts would be rather useless. If, however, the interaction with his work will give rise in your life to an existential quest leading you to a new adventure of faith, with or without the presence of a master, then his effort has not been in vain. Our prayer is that each of you will be in the second category. So help you God!

Dănuț Mănăstireanu

1

The Need to Reconsider Discipleship

More and more important voices in the sphere of Christian theology and spirituality are drawing attention to the fact that, globally, we are undergoing a complex process of transformation which is having a strong impact on those who claim a Christian identity and seek to live it out in a local community. In particular, there is a structural shift in the religious phenomenon itself. Human interest in the religious dimension of life has returned after a period of secularization, but it no longer follows the classical patterns of modernity, which presupposed: a rigorous assumption of a confessional tradition; the importance of the authority of the ecclesial institution; and a high visibility and impact of the Christian church in society. The religious is making a vigorous comeback in people's lives, but in a way that is closer to the spirit of postmodern society, which is interested in local specificity and diversity, in religious experience that responds to particular needs, and in the orientation towards action and experience and less towards cognitive exercise.

Today's society tends to focus on relationships, small communities, and elements of local culture at the expense of the importance of institutions. Christian identity is challenged to respond to a mechanism which is no longer, as in the past, based entirely on tradition, authority and large community projects established in the medium and long term. The social context is highly fragmented and tends to favour a focus on well-defined needs and the specific problems of particular groups of people. For the present and the future, assuming and updating Christian identity requires a continuous process of formation and evaluation in context, according to the needs of the faithful, their social and professional structures, their aspirations, and their expectations. The Christian church is called upon to make a major effort to reconsider its missionary strategies and vision of spirituality. Within this framework, the fundamental value of discipleship as a way of life and as a formative process can support attempts to identify viable solutions. Despite a constant reaction to authority and the classical frameworks of formation and community dynamics, postmodernity represents a new opportunity for discipleship. Christianity is challenged to manifest itself in a context where it can only prevail through authentic models and experiences, not through institutional mechanisms. Discipleship offers the chance to develop a qualitative Christianity that can be presented to this complex world, with different expectations and needs that we didn't know about until recently.

The diversification of the needs of believers calls for a rethinking of the way local churches operate, but this process must consider the danger of Christian communities restructuring into homogeneous social groups. The issue of Christian identity calls increasingly for a coherent formation effort to prepare leaders and mature believers capable of serving in accordance with these demands, and the practice of discipleship is the most comprehensive way in which believers become capable of facing the challenges of today's world. Given the present situation of Christian communities, the importance of a discipleship strategy has become increasingly clear – a strategy that allocates resources to needs-oriented spiritual formation and encourages Christian discipleship, not only as a contextual solution, but also as a fundamental value of Christian spirituality, as a way of life left by Jesus to his church.

Before being a religion, Christianity is a community of people who have decided to follow Jesus Christ, to be his disciples in the world. At the heart of this endeavour is the disciples' desire to be like their master, and the teacher's dedication is meant to support this effort without reservation. Jesus Christ left the church with a very clear mandate to disciple all nations (Matt 28:18–20). He asked the disciples to do exactly what they had seen him do. But it is undeniable that this instruction was not always rigorously followed by Christians. The church has grown in numbers over the centuries, but the way of discipleship has always suffered, especially after Christianity became the accepted religion in the Roman Empire following Emperor Constantine's Edict of Milan (313 AD).

The current situation in the Christian community also suffers in a similar way. Although the practice of discipleship is taken up by churches, it does not appear as a dominant feature of today's spirituality, but rather as an option of a small number of people, being found particularly in monastic circles or in more recent Christian communities which borrow many aspects from the dynamics of social and economic institutions. In the demanding contexts of today's society, such as universities or corporations, the value of apprenticeship has been massively recovered. The results of apprenticeship practice have been well studied by specialists and disseminated in the public space, thus stimulating some local Christian communities to reconsider their own dynamics according to this paradigm. But the inertia of religious institutions continues to show its effects through resistance to change and through non-acceptance of these new challenges. Christian religious leaders are preoccupied with having large numbers of believers, members and sympathizers attending public services, without making discipleship a priority or a fundamental goal of spirituality.

Apprenticeship is an ancient practice found in philosophy, craftsmanship, religious worship, and the military. The basic idea is to help someone get started in a particular field. The biblical term *mathetuo* (to make disciples) has several meanings. One broad meaning is to make followers of Jesus by preaching the gospel (Acts 14:21). Strictly speaking, the word refers to a whole process, such as that described in Matthew 28:19–20, involving several stages: calling, conversion, baptism, teaching, and sending out into the world. Basically, this approach involves retracing the same path that Jesus, in his ministry on earth, followed with his disciples. In the New Testament, there is an equivalence between being a Christian and being a disciple (Acts 11:26). To be a disciple is to assume the condition of one who follows Jesus Christ, one who is willing to accept him as Lord and teacher, as master and authority, in all areas of life. This means keeping his commandments, following his way and example in the world, and bearing his name and mission in history.

Jesus called us to a way of life, not to a new religion or to being followers of a new philosophical trend. He asked his disciples to follow him and to carry his mission forward. Discipleship means first of all a way of life, a complete existence. Therefore Christian spirituality is to be understood as discipleship, that is, an experience of life which involves assuming the values and principles given by Jesus Christ. It is the experience of a complex journey, the adventure of humanity's return to God in an economy of salvation and fulfilment together with the whole creation (Eph 1:10).

Christian discipleship is an ongoing process of transformation according to Christ's model that takes place in a relationship of unconditional obedience to God. Following Christ means fulfilling his mission in the world by serving and loving one's neighbour. Scripture teaches us that the Son of God proclaimed the gospel of the kingdom of heaven, taught people, healed the sick and came to the aid of those in need (Mark 1:21–45). Christ's disciples are called to do all this in the context of today's world. They can fulfil the Christian mandate by being good stewards of creation (respecting the reality of God's work, from the human being to the environment and resources), by participating in the formation of others (in family, profession, ecclesial community, and social community), and by investing in concrete discipleship relationships in various forms and for certain periods of time. Discipleship is not just about striving to be religious beings, people who participate in rites and activities of an ecclesial nature, but it is about assuming and expressing Christian identity in all that we are and do on a daily basis. As disciples of Christ, we are called to carry out the mission entrusted to us through authentic and transformative engagement in profession and social life, in family and local religious community, in politics, the arts, etc.

Reconsidering discipleship also involves an effort to evaluate this experience as we find it in the history of Christianity and in the history of cultures and religions, but especially in the founding experience of the Son of God with his disciples in the short time he worked with them in the world. Thus, the primary referent for any understanding of Christian discipleship remains Scripture, especially the four evangelists' inspired account of the life and mission of Jesus Christ. The next step is to consider how the Twelve carried forward the mandate of their teacher and how exactly discipleship has been passed on from one generation to the next as a fundamental value of the Christian community in the context of the church tradition.

In this book, we propose an exercise in the analysis of discipleship mediated by a reading of the Gospel of Mark. This is not a biblical commentary nor a technical study of the biblical text. Rather, we focus on some passages relevant to the theme of discipleship and try to highlight certain nuances and ingredients of the process while taking into account, as far as possible, some elements specific to this Gospel. Before going into the details of the biblical text, it is helpful to outline the concept of discipleship starting from the theological understanding of what Jesus Christ has accomplished in the world. We also want to distinguish between two expressions of the value of discipleship in Christianity. On the one hand, it should be stressed that every Christian is invited to become a disciple and to live this condition in the world like our Lord and teacher. On the other hand, it should be pointed out that being a disciple of Jesus Christ also requires a kind of commitment to our fellow human beings – an experience of discipleship at the level of the believers. As disciples of Jesus, we are called to participate in the discipleship of others, in the process of becoming disciples of our fellow human beings, of those who have also undertaken to be disciples of the Lord.

Questions

1. How is discipleship practiced in your social context? What are the most visible examples of discipleship in society at large?

2. In these examples, what explains the recovery of this social practice?

3. Can you identify some benefits of the practice of discipleship in these areas?

4. If discipleship is little used in your society, what do you think would be the main explanations?

5. To the extent that there is a certain dynamic of discipleship in your society, in what ways do you think it could give rise to a recovery of discipleship in the Christian environment?

6. To what extent is discipleship happening in your church community?

7. What are the main mechanisms that explain the current reality of discipleship in the Christian community?

8. What arguments do you think would convince a Christian today to engage in a mentoring relationship?

2

Discipleship in the Context of Authority

Discipleship is modelled on the life of Jesus. Discipleship is possible because Jesus Christ inaugurated this reality by what he did as a man and by what he is for us. His whole experience in the world, from birth to ascension, is fundamental for the restoration of humanity and for the possibility of a new way of life. The invitation to become his disciples, to follow his pattern of life, is rooted in all that Jesus Christ, the incarnate Son of God, has achieved. Discipleship is possible because the Son of God himself went through this process. He has restored humanity to the normality of its relationship with God – he has placed human beings under his founding authority. Jesus Christ lived in the world as a person who freely decided to actualize the reason for human existence, as being totally dependent on the creator. Through obedience to God and a life of service and dedication to others, he fulfilled our destiny and brought human beings into the presence of God, to be with him for eternity. What he has achieved is also available to us through our decision to follow him, to be his disciples, to engage in a special relationship with him.

Discipleship is an experience in the context of authority; it involves accepting Christ as the model and example to which we are to relate at all times. Following Christ implies a requirement of obedience and total dependence on him, of accepting his commandments and values as the norms of our life in the world. Jesus tells us that all authority has been given to him in heaven and on earth (Matt 28:18–21) and it is within this framework that the life of believers and the economy of salvation unfold. This is the foundation on which the call of people to become disciples and to make disciples for the kingdom of God is based.

The Anthropological and Christological Basis of Discipleship

God's authority is what makes becoming – that is, human development – possible. The etymology of the Latin word *auctoritas* indicates that authority is what makes one grow and develop (see 1 Cor 3:7). In Christian anthropology, it is accepted that becoming and change is constitutive of human nature and of created reality as a whole (the idea is developed by the earliest Christian theologians such as Theophilus of Antioch and Irenaeus of Lyons). This becoming of human beings is a continuous process of transformation leading to a purpose or destiny of its own. According to Christian revelation, the dynamism of human life is aimed at union with God, humans being created to share in divine goodness, in communion with the divine persons for eternity (Eph 1:10).

Authority ensures becoming, and implies a relationship between the one who becomes and the one who manages and makes possible the process of change. But the relationship of authority is only validated in the space of freedom (Gal 4:6, 7). The human being is transformed into the likeness of God by exercising his or her own freedom (2 Cor 3:17–18), always moving towards a state of maturity that leaves room for communion with divine persons and participation in what Christ has accomplished for us (Eph 4:13–15). The destiny of the human being to be united with God for eternity is possible as a result of this transformative dynamic on the basis of authority and freedom. The process of becoming involves humanity's personal mode of existence and takes the form of an ongoing exercise of relating to God and to others, a continuous experience of actualizing the potential received at creation (the image of God) in order to attain the likeness of God and the experience of eternal life (Rom 6:22).

In human experience, authority implies a relationship of mutual recognition between human beings and God. First, human persons recognize that the source of their life is the creator and that without a constant and solid relationship with him, they cannot have life, being, and movement (Acts 17:28). Second, divine persons recognize human beings as persons in the process of becoming Christlike (Eph 4:13). The triune God relates to humans not only as a result of his creative work, but also as persons whom he loves and desires to become his children for eternity. The exercise of divine authority over human beings requires this recognition of God's sovereignty: humanity's freedom to accept the terms of the relationship with the divine being as the source of existence and becoming. Thus, the relations in this dynamic of authority are asymmetrical. It is God who holds the authority and is the source of all becoming. Human beings sdefine their identity and the normality of their existence to the extent that they remain in a relationship of obedience and total dependence on their creator. Maintaining these coordinates implies that human beings remain within the limits of their own freedom and destiny. This type of relationship does not, however, cancel out the possibility of love and interpersonal communion. The fullness of the relationship between the creator and created beings is made clearer because one of the divine persons has become like us, our equal. The incarnation of the Son of God is not only the framework for the full realization of the relationship between the human being and the creator, but also the foundation for a new kind of relationship with the divinity to which we have access as sons of God (Rom 8:14–15).

We can thus appreciate that the becoming of humanity has its counterpart in another becoming, that of the Son of God. He accomplishes a *kenosis* (Phil 2:7), a descent, a passage from what he was (God) to what he was not (man). This dynamic also involves an exercise of freedom in the context of authority. The Son submits to the Father, in the process of incarnation (John 5:19). He assumes his human nature and obeys God the Father in all things. The assumption of this mode of existence makes possible the healing of the human being, its repositioning in a proper position in relation to God. In this way, Christ becomes the first human being who restores the authentic bond with God (Eph 4:24) and repositions the coordinates of the exercise of divine authority in the life of the human person, an authority that produces becoming towards union with God.

A fundamental consequence of the incarnation is that we had among us a human person who lived life fully at the level of the created being, that is, led humanity to an existence in accordance with the meaning and destiny received from God in the beginning. This becoming of the Son in humanity meant at the same time a becoming of the human, a profound change at the ontological level, that is, a transformation of his mode of existence, a transition from a failed mode of existence to a fulfilled, true one (2 Cor 5:17, 21). Thus, in Jesus Christ we have with us and in us the restored man, the human person who has situated himself within the parameters of a normal and failure-free existence (Rom 6:9), of a dynamic that unfolds according to the reason for being received from the creator.

The incarnate Son of God lives as a full human being in a relationship of authority with God and becomes a founding authority of new life for every human being who accepts him as master and brother. The beneficiaries of this process of change and re-establishment in the direction of God's destiny are the disciples, those who enter into a relationship of authority with Christ. Accepting the process of discipleship or following Jesus Christ in all aspects of life involves a line of demarcation, a decision to move from a fallen way of life to an authentic one (Rom 6:6–11). What then follows is a journey of growth toward maturity (Col 1:28), a transformational effort that has as its endpoint the union with God. Discipleship is the action of continual change of a person who has accepted entry into a relationship with Christ as master and model. It is a process that begins with the decision to reorient oneself and place oneself under the authority of Jesus Christ for life (John 12:26).

Coordinates of Authority and Discipleship

In summary, we speak of authority as what produces becoming, and as the founding relationship that ensures the dynamics of the process of transformation of human beings towards the goal of their perfection. It is important to note first how this process was carried out in the life of Jesus Christ, as it is presented synthetically in the biblical text, both in the Gospels and in the well known christological hymn of Philippians 2:5–11. From these passages some defining elements of authority in the life of Christ stand out, elements that we will outline below.

Authority Is Received

God has the supreme, founding authority par excellence, the only absolute intrinsic authority, and the only source of authority. Every other authority in the world is a delegated one, because it is received from him. In the economy of creation and salvation, Jesus Christ assumes a well-defined role and places himself under the authority of the Father (Heb 5:5–9). He decides to obey God unconditionally, to the end, in all aspects of his life (Phil 2:8). Everything that the Son of God accomplishes in the world always presupposes reference to the Father as the authority, as the personal presence that makes it possible to become and to achieve all the proposed objectives. It is also very important to note that the whole of Jesus's life is realized in the economy of the Holy Spirit (Luke 4:1, 14), under the authority of this person who was always manifested in what the incarnate Son has said or done in history. At the same time, the biblical text shows us that the mission of Jesus implies a mandate, a sending, and an empowerment with authority from God for what he has to do. Jesus's life highlights a fundamental principle for the experience of discipleship: to be an authority is to be under authority (John 5:25–30). Christ places himself in a relationship of authority under God in order to benefit from his action and to be himself in authority over people. In reading the Gospel, it is important to note how this principle worked in the life of Jesus from the beginning of his ministry to its end.

Authority Is Earned

Jesus comes into the world as sent by the Father, as one invested by God with authority to do his will (John 12:49–50). But the exercise of this authority requires a free personal assumption of mission and a continuing decision to move forward despite the obstacles and limitations of human existence in the world. Even for the Son of God, it was not enough to receive authority, to be invested and sent into the world. It required a personal assumption and confirmation of this authority through a way of life, through all his decisions and actions. One's manifested authority is gained by consistent obedience to the founding authority (Heb 4:14–16), by constant reference to the being that can ensure the consistency of one's identity and mission. Jesus earned his authority over people by his pattern of life, by his obedience and service, by the way he placed himself under God's authority and the fulfilment of his plan (John 17:1–8). Jesus became an intrinsic authority and model for us precisely because he demonstrated the quality of a life and mission that God validated as authentic and the source of change for all people (Phil 2:9–11). In this capacity, he helps our becoming, he is our referent and model that encourages us to follow his example. We can thus underline another essential principle for discipleship: namely that the master or teacher, because he has acquired or gained authority, can thus gather disciples because he has something to offer, and the relationship with him is a source of change.

Authority Produces Results

Jesus was then and is now an authority for his disciples because his life model and his presence in the world have brought and continues to bring concrete results, generating becoming. Christ worked on himself and on people; he brought his own experience to completion and became a model for others (Col 1:18–20). But this achievement is not an end in itself. He remains an authority because he constantly offers himself to those who need him, assisting us as a transforming presence, as a relationship that realigns all things in our lives, as the engine of human dynamics towards our destiny (Eph 4:15–16). The salvation of the whole world is possible today as a result of what Christ is and has accomplished. But access to his work necessarily implies entering into a relationship of discipleship with him, accepting his authority (Luke 9:23). Christ's work and his authority are carried forward into the world through his disciples, through their life and ministry. The disciples have been commissioned to do this, and their action implies that they themselves become models, authorities, and examples that produce transformation in others (Matt

5:13–16). We therefore stress a third principle of Christian discipleship: the authority of the master produces becoming, brings consistency, and gives authority to his disciples (John 15:16). The process of discipleship creates inter-human relationships that are based on the founding and transforming authority of Jesus Christ to change people's lives.

This framework thus outlined applies first to the relationship between each person and Jesus, and then to strictly human relationships, in which some become disciples and others guide them. The most important thing to emphasize is that Christian discipleship or the Christian life as discipleship is possible because Jesus has become an authority over all creation (Col 1:18). It is from this position that he makes it possible for us to take on the task of being his disciples. The Christian's condition in the world remains always the same to the end and cannot change. Believers in Jesus Christ are disciples, no matter how far they have travelled and how much they can help others. This is encouraging and gives us hope that we always have his assistance and authority with us, along with his love and friendship (John 17:25–26). Likewise, the disciple of Jesus in the world follows his example and is ready to disciple others, to be an occasion of transformation and maturity. Discipleship among people is important because it gives us the opportunity to make available to our neighbours what we gain from our relationship with Christ. Likewise, being Jesus's disciples is always confirmed by being servants of those whom the Son of God came to serve (Mark 10:43–45). We are called to disciple others to the extent that we assume and maintain our identity as disciples of the Lord. To be authorities for our neighbours and to serve them in their becoming means to put people in relationship with Christ and to make his founding authority shine through us. We can only offer to others what we have received from him, what we have become as a result of accepting him as Lord and teacher.

Conclusion

The Gospels document the whole process of Jesus's becoming and the journey of his relationship with his disciples. The other books of the New Testament show us how the transforming authority of Christ's person and life was carried forward. From there we can glean teachings and principles of discipleship as a way of life as lived out by our master and his disciples, and we can intuit ways to place them in the context of our present experience. Perhaps some readers of the sacred text wonder why we have four Gospels instead of one, why it was necessary to present the life of Jesus from several perspectives. The answer may seem more obvious if we accept that both the personality of Jesus and what he accomplished in the world are extremely complex realities. The authors of the Gospels, even though there are four of them, do not attempt to exhaust this complexity, but rather to suggest it and invite us to pay attention to it. By its very nature, as a divine-human product, the biblical text is always open and full of unsuspected depths and at the same time reveals very clear, pertinent, unequivocal truths.

The inheritance left by Jesus Christ is not a set of doctrines that had to be written down precisely by his disciples, but a real life lived in the world that had fundamental implications for the destiny of humanity and the entire cosmos. As witnesses to this reality, the authors of the Gospels provide us with the coordinates of this authentic experience of what the Son of God accomplished, but as individuals who themselves benefited from the transforming action of Christ's work. Analysing the Gospels in order to capture the dynamics of discipleship is not an easy task and requires an effort to understand the nuances of each author, to get to grips with the perspective with which he approaches the life and personality of Jesus. It is clear that analysing the theme of discipleship in each Gospel is a distinct adventure worth undertaking. We decided to do this exercise on the text of Mark for several reasons that will be discussed in the next section.

Questions

1. What is your first reaction to hearing the term "authority"?
2. What patterns of authority can you identify in your own life (family, school, church, society)?
3. How have these influenced your understanding of God's authority?
4. How does your church community understand the manifestation of God's authority?
5. To what extent does your personal relationship to Christ's authority determine your acceptance of authority at the human level?
6. How do Christians in your church community relate to civil authority?
7. How does your church community understand the manifestation of human authority in the context of the church?
8. How might we argue the importance of an authority such as that of a spiritual father in the life of the believer?

3

The Theme of Discipleship in the Gospel of Mark

As expert studies point out, the Gospel of Mark is chronologically the first of four such biblical texts, written sometime before Jerusalem was destroyed by the Roman imperial armies, between 65 and 70 AD. In style, the book is quite different from the other two synoptic texts (the Gospels of Matthew and Luke). It has a narrative emphasis that particularly highlights the actions of Jesus, and the tone is alert and dramatic. The figure of Christ emerges more from his active presence than from speeches, the author emphasising his strength of character and even the mystery of his personality.

Beyond the central figure of Jesus and the specifics of his mission, commentators point out that the theme of discipleship is readily discernible in this Gospel. The evangelist Mark is the first biblical author to give us an account of the disciples of Jesus, and he does so in a distinctive way. The narrative dynamics of the text highlight the presence of the disciples alongside Jesus from the first to the last chapter of the book. Jesus acts, gestures, and speaks, but he is always involved on two fronts. One relates to the masses of people he addresses from time to time, and the other concerns the disciples, those who have gathered around him and follow him everywhere. If we accept that this theme is highlighted in the Gospel of Mark, then we can seek to follow, throughout the book, the dynamics of the relationship between Jesus and his disciples, so that we can thus observe the details, nuances, stakes, and tensions of the discipleship process, as provided by the divinely inspired biblical author. The aim of this exercise is to understand the discipleship process as best we can in the light of the elements we can extract from this book of Scripture. Without claiming to be an expert exegetical study, we will go through the Gospel as a reader familiar with the biblical text, but who is interested in observing how

Mark presents Jesus's relationship with his followers. This approach involves first outlining how Christ carries out his mission and how it affects the disciples in the process. Then, the idea is to observe the response and the participation of the disciples in this setting created by Christ for them.

To begin with, however, it is important to point out a few elements that may be considered technical, but which are specific to this Gospel in relation to the theme under study. We consider first the terms used in the text to designate those who follow Jesus. Throughout the book, Mark prefers to use the terms disciples (*mathetai*) and the Twelve (*dodeka*) for their small circle. In contrast to the Synoptics, the evangelist uses the term apostles (*apostolous*) only once (in Mark 6:30). In order to underline the dynamic of the discipleship process, the New Testament also uses a specific verb (*akoloutheo*) to designate the action of following Jesus, of always being with him. In this Gospel, disciples are those who follow Jesus, those who accompany him everywhere. But the biblical text distinguishes between two categories of people who followed Christ: (1) the crowds attracted by his teaching and miracles; and (2) a small group who identify themselves as his disciples. So, the very fact of following Jesus is not enough. Discipleship involves following Jesus in the sense of appropriating his model of life, his values, and principles, not merely following him through the Jewish cities.

Compared to the other Gospels, it seems that Mark most frequently uses the phrase "the Twelve" to refer to the group of those chosen by Jesus to be his disciples. The title seems to be consistent with the author's emphasis on the authority with which the Lord's disciples were invested and their special role in the Christian community which formed after Jesus's ascension to heaven. As will become established in New Testament thought, the Twelve represent a fundamental institution for the church, the foundation on which the body of Christ is built in the world. If this is a specific emphasis of Mark's Gospel, we will need to follow it throughout the text and point out possible implications for the dimension of authority for Christian discipleship, especially that related to passing on the true identity of Jesus.

The Twelve are presented by the evangelist Mark as people with weaknesses and troubles, frequently unable to understand who their master is and what he is doing, traits that place them almost at the antithesis of the position of authority with which they were invested, and their proximity to the person of Jesus. This is another aspect of the book's specific treatment of discipleship that is worth exploring. We will consider how the Gospel text highlights Jesus's willingness to address the disciples privately, to take into account all their fears, misunderstandings and weaknesses. Through this strategy, the Gospel of Mark may be trying to emphasize that the apostles are not superhumans, and their special choice does not spare them the effort of important transformations in their lives and personalities. Rather, the disciples' journey with Jesus is a paradigmatic one, as is the message about people's relationship with Christ that is offered to the community of believers of all times and in all geographical spaces. Equally, this Gospel shows us how Jesus does not spare his disciples, does not isolate them from the wider community in which they find themselves, and reveals how their identity, constructed in the Jewish social and religious context, is now undergoing a harsh process of evaluation and transformation. It is precisely this difficult approach to analysing a confused Jewish identity in Jesus's time that is highlighted and seems to be a very important one in the economy of the Gospel of Mark.

Another element that is worth highlighting about the particularity of this Gospel is that discipleship is presented not only with a great deal of realism, but also with a number of specific elements concerning the disciple's ability to assume the way of the master. These aspects seem particularly important for the book's original recipients, most likely Christians in a period of persecution and suffering, but they remain valid for the rest of Christian history. For Mark the Evangelist, true discipleship involves the capacity to assume Jesus's condition in the world, regardless of time and context, regardless of dangers and challenges. Following Christ means actualizing his values and mission, being ready to live them regardless of the consequences and the reaction of others. The disciples of Jesus must demonstrate their ability to fundamentally change their way of life, identity, thinking, and behaviour. Often, this change is radical and requires a very great effort, almost beyond human capabilities. The Gospel takes this idea to its logical conclusion and asks the disciples to renounce themselves completely and to be ready for sacrifice and even martyrdom. But this condition of the disciple does not refer only to the apostolic age or to the period of persecution of the church, but is also valid today, when there is freedom to manifest faith as we wish. It seems that embracing the path of discipleship does not exempt us from direct confrontation with a series of obstacles that are related both to the state of humanity affected by the fall and to the socio-cultural conditions of the context in which we live.

In parallel with the realism of the process that Jesus's chosen disciples go through, Mark's Gospel also subtly brings into the picture a number of atypical disciples, either from the Judean or Gentile crowd, people who appear at interesting moments and do things that were expected to come from those in Jesus's inner circle. We notice a surprising dimension of discipleship from a distance, with people appearing out of nowhere and making substantial gestures. This openness to unconventional disciples is suggested by the biblical text and raises a number of questions about divine economy in the world, the dynamics of discipleship and the risks of a static, context-dependent view. The text invites us to reflect on the idea that, either in Jesus's times or now, there is no monopoly of the church or of certain people in the church on truth and discipleship, that we can always be surprised by God's economy through unexpected people and circumstances. Like Jesus's disciples of the past, Christians today may be blind to certain realities, may ignore certain horizons of divine presence in the world, and may have unfounded expectations that all things revolve around them.

There is another point to be observed in this Gospel. It is the way in which Mark the Evangelist presents the disciples in the tension of Jesus's confrontations with the Jewish leaders of the time and with the authorities of the unseen and evil world. The biblical text seems to alternate and replay several times the theme of these confrontations. In such contexts, the true identity of Jesus is called into question. We must not forget that the Gospel of Mark insists on this identity with nuances that were related to its audience and to the specific problems faced by Christians at that time. The Gospel, therefore, demands of us a twofold effort: to grasp the questions and dilemmas facing the disciples of Jesus, in accordance with the problems raised by the context of the first century; and to take into account the situations facing the disciples of Christ in a totally different setting, such as the present one. Relating to the identity of Jesus is fundamental to defining the identity of the disciple and to the assumption and manifestation of that status in the world. Interestingly, Mark leaves open many details of how the disciples approach the identity of their master, as well as the challenges Jesus brings to their understanding of him. Also, the Twelve are always in the crosshairs of religious leaders and certain prominent people in society because of their association with their teacher and the confusion that frequently hovers over his identity.

A very important point for the evangelist Mark is to draw attention to the fact that both the people and their leaders, and the disciples, only partially understood the nature of Jesus's message and mission. Many of the events concerning the life and ministry of Jesus in this Gospel are presented in relation to the disciples. The biblical author is interested in showing us the attitudes of the disciples, how they understood and responded to the words and actions of their teacher. If we can speak of a tension curve in this book, it can be identified at the level of how the disciples understand who Jesus Christ is. If at the beginning the biblical text often signals the disciples' puzzlement and questioning about who Jesus is, a climax of this line is precisely the moment when the teacher asks the disciples what they think about his identity. The text does not dwell much on Peter's clarifying answer, nor on the implications of this knowledge, but it is clear that this message plays a very important role in the Gospel. The apostle Peter utters a revealing message about who Jesus really is even before his suffering in Jerusalem. This clarification of the identity of the one who died and rose again is central to the Christian faith and to the life of the disciple of Christ. Even though the disciples were seriously challenged by what they believed and understood about Jesus, the biblical revelation that he is the promised Christ, the Son of Man and the Son of God remains the central reference by which his life and mission in the world must be understood.

With these introductory elements, we will go through the Gospel of Mark, and we will stop in a few places that we consider representative of the theme under consideration. The approach aims at selecting some nuances and suggestions with fertile potential for the understanding of discipleship in today's world, while avoiding more technical exegetical analyses or incursions into the cultural-historical context of the period in which Jesus and his disciples lived.

Questions

1. How much attention is given to the topic of discipleship in sermons or teaching events in the church to which you belong? Can you give some examples of ideas about discipleship that you frequently hear in church?

2. How current and important is this theme to the believers with whom you are in contact? Do you know people who say they are in an discipleship relationship?

3. To what extent do you think someone can have a discipleship relationship with Jesus just by reading a Gospel?

4. Could one imagine a discipleship relationship from a distance? If so, how?

5. Is it obvious from the Gospel text that the Christian life involves a process of discipleship? If so, is it still necessary for the church to insist on explaining it?

4

The Master's Entry on the Scene

It is specific to the Gospel of Mark that the description of the identity of Jesus Christ is made without any reference to his birth and childhood. It begins abruptly with the context of the beginning of his mission. In a very condensed manner, as if in a rush to set Jesus in action, a succession of events is presented, events which are given ample space in the other Gospels: the mission of John the Baptist and the baptism of the Jews at the river Jordan (Mark 1:1–8); the baptism of Jesus himself and the witness of the Father in heaven (Mark 1:9–11); the period of forty days in the wilderness where he was tempted by Satan (Mark 1:12–13); and the imprisonment of John the Baptist and Jesus's decision to begin his own public mission (Mark 1:14–15). In this introductory overview, Jesus's identity is quickly sketched out in a few clear outlines, typical for biblical language and for the context of that time. First, we note a series of significant names and appellatives: Christ (the anointed one, Messiah); Son of God; the one who is mightier than John; beloved Son; Jesus of Nazareth. We are also given the key witnesses or references confirming Jesus's identity: Scripture, by reference to the book of Isaiah; John the Baptist; God himself, through the voice of the Father in heaven; and the visible presence of the Holy Spirit.

On the one hand, all of this introduces Jesus to the stage in the spirit of Old Testament Scripture and the Jewish expectation of the fulfilment of God's promises. On the other hand, these elements respond to the need of the first-century Christian community for clarification about the person of Jesus. Without insisting on these points of reference, however, the evangelist invites the reader to see who Jesus is from the perspective of his ministry and from the way he lived in the world. It is interesting to note a few details of how the evangelist sets the stage for Christ, the disciple-maker, our Lord and teacher.

First of all, Jesus is called in the introduction of the Gospel the one who "comes after" John – the one who follows the prophet. This image already sets the theme of discipleship at the beginning of the book. Jesus's identity is confirmed by an authority – a prophet of the Lord – whom Christ respects and obeys. Jesus follows John not only in the logic of a temporal succession, but of a mandate and confirmation that he receives publicly from God through his servant. Even if the biblical text is only allusive and things are presented synthetically, this aspect is essential for the theme of discipleship. Jesus fully assumes the terms of God's economy and thus ensures continuity. His identity and ministry are not confirmed in the institutional context of the age, but they receive their legitimacy in the spirit of Scripture and within a fully validated public mission. For Jesus's disciples of all times, it is very important to emphasize this truth. The new teacher in Judea does not appear out of nowhere and is not an illegitimate authority without authentic witness from God and the people. He does not emerge as a reaction to a corrupt system, as a revolutionary who wants to correct a system eroded to the maximum, or as an alternative to formal leadership, having no intrinsic authority. On the contrary, Jesus is first willing to follow the one invested by God and set to inaugurate the work of the gospel. We could say that Jesus is first and foremost an obedient disciple who stands in the continuity of the work of the one who opened the way and who has already received recognition from God and the Jewish people. Mark the Evangelist points out that the people of Judea and Jerusalem came to John and confessed their sins and were baptized in the water of Jordan. At his peak, when his message and mission are at their most visible point, the prophet John announces the appearance of another prophet, another teacher to succeed him. The moment that attests to Jesus's recognition of John's authority and compliance is when Jesus comes to the prophet and accepts his baptism as any other member of the people.

Second, it is essential to consider the significance of Jesus's gesture of receiving John's baptism. Through this act, Christ affirms his solidarity with those whom he is ready to serve, to share their experience and destiny. The future teacher is a man fully aware of his need for God and participates unreservedly in his economy in the world. Even though John announces Jesus as one who is greater and more powerful than himself, with a more important ministry in God's plan, Jesus does not take all this for granted. He does not appear on the scene as an individual from a superior race, as a saint or a chosen one who comes to care for the insignificant and sinful. Jesus does not place himself on a pedestal, from which to demand obedience and compliance. Through baptism, Christ confirms that he is one like us, in solidarity with us in all things and willing to serve us, to be the engine of a new experience in which we can all be part. Our master and teacher is one of us, ready to rise up and fulfil the mission entrusted to him, aware that this is only possible in the logic of providence, that is, of legitimacy and continuity, of dependence on God and obedience, of service out of love and in freedom. Jesus accepts the baptism of repentance and forgiveness of sins and thus can himself be the one who continues the mission begun by John. He is the disciple who goes through the fundamental experience of taking the human condition to the end, expressing the need for God and salvation. Jesus shows submission to God's authority by accepting obedience to his servants, and he highlights the central theme of his mission, because he accepts God's call for all people to be reconciled with divinity. By obeying John the Baptist and his ministry, the Son of God demonstrates that he has agreed to live within the normal frameworks of human existence, that he knows how to recognize the divine authority vested in the prophets and the authentic people of faith. Only in this way can he become the master who will carry forward the message of conversion, of the good news of the kingdom of God. As a man capable of recognizing God's authority in others, Jesus confirms his own identity and his capacity for service, that he can be of service to others and is ready to serve through self-sacrifice and discipleship.

Third, water baptism is the occasion for a deeper experience that becomes the basis for his special mission in the world, namely to baptize people in the Holy Spirit. Even though the biblical text does not use the expression as such in the case of Jesus, it seems that the experience after coming out of the water of the Jordan refers to what John the Baptist announces about Christ's mission. As a human being, the Son of God is first baptized in the Holy Spirit, and so accepts that he will manifest himself in the world in total dependence on the ministry of this divine person who offers life and communion with God to all. Mark the Evangelist points out that the work of Jesus marks a major step, an improvement on that of the prophet John. But this was not possible without Jesus himself having passed through the economy of the Holy Spirit. What he experienced as a human being, what he became through the work of the Spirit beginning at the Jordan, is a fundamental experience that he is now ready to share with everyone. In the spirit of Scripture, Jesus becomes the Spirit-filled servant of God, that is, the human being in deep communion with God, living in his will and love. The fullness of the Spirit is the full expression of the kingdom of God, the fulfilment of humanity's destiny. The Gospel text also mentions that what Jesus experienced at the Jordan culminates in a confirmation of his identity by God in a message, in a voice that calls him the Son of God, the beloved, the one in whom God finds all his pleasure. In this very synthetic and dense way, the Gospel portrays our Lord and teacher in the process of his own becoming. It is a founding experience that shows us a man being passed through the economy of God, who first lives in himself a foundational experience for humanity and then receives a mission, along with the authority necessary to fulfill it. Jesus is God's servant, full of the Holy Spirit, ready to carry out what he has been entrusted with, carrying on the work of the prophets and great men of faith.

Fourth, the one baptized and confirmed by the prophet John undergoes a period of testing and evaluation. Mark gives no details on how Jesus was tempted by Satan during the forty days in the wilderness, nor does he give the reason for it. We know from the book of Job, for example, that Satan is always an agent of accusation, who blames human beings before God and demands validation of their quality by hard tests. We can intuit, then, that we are dealing with an evaluative exercise that concerns both Jesus's new identity and the beginning of his mission. It is suggestive that Mark the Evangelist uses an expression that shows the imminence of this phase and its relation to the previous one: it states that immediately after baptism the Spirit takes the initiative and leads Jesus in this direction. Both the wilderness theme and the period of forty days have a rich symbolic significance in the Scriptures. One can think of Israel and all the trials it went through after the exit from Egypt, the personified presence of evil that opposes God's will, etc. For the theme of discipleship, it is important to stress that in Jesus we have a genuine master who has gone through all the trials and temptations to which a human is subject in the world. He has legitimacy in what he says and asks of his disciples, he is a valid and worthy model to follow because he has gone through this hard school of trials and temptations and has come through it well. Before Jesus became a teacher and guide to others, he was an obedient disciple, a dutiful servant who diligently went through his lessons. He has thus earned the authority to lead his disciples along the path of formation and towards God.

For the period that follows, when we see him in action and when he begins to disciple people, all these aspects of Jesus's identity and his journey to becoming a master are very important. They are an essential moral foundation for the disciple who has decided to believe in Jesus, as well as a vital support for those who have themselves come to disciple others. Following Christ involves accepting all the stages he has gone through, especially that of acquiring and strengthening his position as our authority, Lord and teacher. This transparency of Scripture about the process of Jesus's becoming is determinative of authentic faith and courageous engagement in discipleship. What he acquired is essential for us and represents a foundation, a legacy that is accessible to us today through his presence and ongoing mission with his disciples in the world.

Questions

1. There is a perception that mentors are hard to find in churches today. Why do you think this happens?

2. Do you have or have you ever had a mentor? If so, how did this relationship come about and how did it develop?

3. If not, what are the reasons for the lack of a mentoring experience in your life?

4. What does the ideal mentor look like for you and what do you most want from a mentor?

5. What are the biggest fears of Christians today in terms of engaging in a mentoring relationship?

6. Is there someone you consider a model worth following in your life? What in particular has caught your attention about that person?

7. How appealing do you think is the person of Jesus as a model mentor for the contemporary Christian?

5

Calling the Disciples

Jesus's initiative to recruit his disciples, recounted in the very first chapter of Mark's Gospel (Mark 1:16–20), opens the discussion on discipleship. This call of the disciples must be seen and understood, however, in the context of the mission of the teacher. We have here an apocalyptic setting (Mark 1:15). Jesus's work begins with preaching the gospel, the good news from God. The biblical sentence refers to the book of the prophet Isaiah (52:7), the good news from God announcing salvation through his sovereignty reigning over all. This salvation is promised to the people of Israel and to all nations (Isa 60–61). The biblical author emphasizes that the time of salvation has arrived, that God's reign and kingdom are becoming manifest in the world through the work of Christ. Jesus's proclamation includes two very important elements. The first concerns the time, the right time (*kairos*) for action. The Saviour's message announces a fulfilment of the times, namely that we have entered the decisive period of history in which God fulfils what he has promised. The good news is taking shape in the world, God is taking action and offering his salvation to all people. The Son of God's entrance onto the stage of the divine economy represents the fulfilment of the biblical prophecies that history is reaching its critical moment, its period of greatest importance. The beginning of Jesus's mission coincides with this inauguration of the apocalyptic age, the age in which God's authority over history is expressed in all its sovereignty. The second part of Jesus's message concerns the human's attitude and response to God's initiative. Two specific verbs express the divine expectation for those who hear the good news: to repent and to believe. The promised salvation and the restoration of God's kingdom presuppose the profound act of changing one's way of thinking and living (*metanoia*) and then holding these coordinates in a deep relationship with God in the hope that this process of human restoration will be accomplished for everyone. Believing means the commitment of the human being, in its totality, to the experience of the divine process of salvation, a concrete participation in God's economy in the world, a willing acceptance of the coordinates in which this transformation of human life is effectively realized.

The calling of the first disciples takes place within this framework of the development of the ministry of salvation which has Jesus Christ at its centre. The good news from God is called by Mark "The gospel of Jesus Christ" (Mark 1:1). He is the Son of God through whom all that is promised is fulfilled. He is therefore the reference point to which people are called to refer in the process of repentance and in expressing their faith. God's expectation is that all will turn to Christ, will enter into a relationship with him, and will accept him as their teacher and saviour. The call of the first disciples is paradigmatic and responds to this demand to relate to Jesus. First, in order to benefit from God's salvation – participation in his life for eternity – people must become disciples of Jesus and follow him all their lives. That is why Jesus says to the two brothers, the first to be called, Andrew and Peter, "follow me" (Mark 1:17). To be a disciple of Jesus means to be with him, to assume a new identity and a new way of life, in line with what the teacher has shown us about living in the world. Then, following Jesus means being "fishers of men," that is, being partners and effective participants in his mission. Authentic disciples are those who continue Christ's work in the world, who put into practice the values and principles of his teaching. The most obvious element in Mark 1 is the connection or continuity between the nature of the gospel proclaimed by Jesus and the concrete invitation to people to follow him. God inaugurates the eschatological times and sends his Son into the world, but this reality takes shape and settles into the reality of the world through a dialogue with human beings. After revealing his plans, God leaves room for human freedom and response. Mark's way of presenting this invitation draws our attention to a few details on which we dwell below.

First, we notice the visual, scenic, almost photographic dimension of the biblical text. The author frequently points out that Jesus saw things and then acted. In the case of the call of the first four disciples, Mark offers no details indicating that Jesus spoke to them or did anything special to persuade these fishermen to follow him. The biblical text insists on the idea that the teacher saw them at work (casting nets into the sea or repairing gear) and extended the invitation, and they left their work and went to him. The scene itself highlights the contrast between the lives of the disciples before and after the call. The fishermen's gesture of leaving their gear and their work indicates a radical relocation, a change that engulfs their whole life. We are witnessing a decision and an action to leave everything behind. The response of those called upon is not a verbal reaction that comes from an overheard speech, it is not an intellectual adherence to a body of knowledge, but a decision that changes the fundamentals of their previous existence. According to Mark, the fishermen seem to respond immediately, without a second thought, in accordance with the urgency suggested by the message with which Christ begins his mission: "the time is fulfilled," history has entered a straight line towards its climax, and God offers humans the chance to participate in what is already happening through the presence of his Son in the world. We could say that discipleship presupposes this clear and profound human response, the prompt attitude and readiness to fundamentally change the coordinates of everyday life. The following of Christ is based on the understanding that at the heart of history essential things are happening because the world has received into it God himself who become man, and that this presence is a transforming and restorative one for all who enter into a relationship with him. The urgency of the human being's response is not a hasty act, or a decision made in the heat of the moment under the pressure of a message or emotion, but derives from the gravity and seriousness of the need to find solutions and answers to fundamental questions, which are meaningful to our existence.

Second, Mark severely limits Jesus's speech and action in this scene. The disciples hear a simple message saying "follow me." It seems that this is the essential element here – to be invited, to be addressed by the master, and, in this case, by God incarnate. Here we have a clear allusion to the ancient context where, among both Jews and Greco-Romans, the master-disciple relationship was of paramount importance. Christianity implies the constant reiteration of this invitation, this decisive gesture of God addressing humans and respecting their freedom of decision. This picture of the calling of the first disciples reminds us of a similar scene in the Old Testament (1 Kgs 19:19–20). The prophet Elijah chooses his disciple who is working in the field. He does this without speaking, without explanation, rather by a symbolic gesture: he places his mantle on the disciple's shoulders. The response is immediate. Elisha leaves his work, his parents and his home and follows his master into the Lord's service. Similarly, in the case of the fishermen, when the teacher makes the call, the disciples respond, ready for action. They seem to have sensed the importance of the gesture of being invited to be disciples of Jesus; they seem to be ready for this encounter. There is an old saying that "when the disciple is ready, the master appears." The Gospel pericope does not give us any details about the possible preparation and what it would entail. It does not tell us how prepared the disciples were and whether they had any information about Jesus's identity or God's plan with the people of Israel. But it does record the effect of the call, the promptness of the response and the reversal that occurs. It is possible that the original recipients of this Gospel needed such a density of biblical message, a picture that captures the decisive role of Jesus's call and the reorientation of the being of the disciple who agrees to follow him. Perhaps today's reader also needs such a perspective.

Finally, just as laconically, the biblical text stresses a new identity for the disciples. Suggestively, starting from the status and profession of the disciples, Jesus promises a becoming that makes them fit for a special mission. The phrase "fishers of men" (Mark 1:17) is not accidental. On the one hand, it refers to the constitution and character of those chosen by Jesus, and on the other hand, to a symbolic charge that has a long spiritual tradition. The idea of fishing for people is not new. In the Platonic tradition it appears with the meaning of seeking disciples, of creating master-teacher relationships. The theme is also present in Jewish spirituality – we find the idea in the prophets, where God is presented as a fisher of men, but also in relationships between believers, as the prophet Jeremiah suggests (Jer 16), or as the phrase was used in the community of Qumran. In the New Testament, the first fisher of men is Jesus. He seeks out his disciples and invites them to follow him, to enter a process of becoming and building a new identity. The goal of discipleship is for disciples to become like their master. Jesus tells them from the outset what his expectations are, what they are called to become. The phrase used by Jesus suggests that discipleship is not an end in itself. It is a tool, a means by which people are transformed, and become mature continuators of their teacher's work. For disciples, being fishers of people means that one day they will be in Jesus's position and be able to call others to be disciples. On his departure from this world, Christ leaves the Twelve with this mandate, to go out into the world to disciple the Gentiles, that is, to do what they saw him do. The dynamics of God's work in the world presupposes this close connection between generations, this ongoing process of investing in people, of making them fit to carry on the life and mission of Jesus. Fortunately, the teacher did not leave behind a formal religious institution or system to ensure this. He left the honest and transparent pattern of his own experience with his disciples; he left a value system, an understanding of the nature of reality and of God, a coherent message, and a way forward for his disciples to achieve their eternal destiny. All of this was lived and shaped into his concrete life and that of his disciples in the Jewish context of the ancient world. His desire was that this model, this strategy, should continue from one generation to the next, in new contexts, with different people, with specific problems, but with the same stake and the same purpose.

These specific elements of Jesus's call remain valid for all times and places. People are called to become disciples of Christ and to respond to God's invitation to assume a new identity and a new way of life in the world. The importance of the invitation derives from what God has already accomplished for us through the life of his Son in the world. History has been given new coordinates, and the divine economy contains this open invitation to salvation, healing and transformed life for all people and for the whole of created reality. The human response to this call is essential, and God awaits for it with great interest. Following Jesus and becoming his disciple means taking up the mission of the teacher and carrying it forward in all cultures and in all times. The choice and decision to become a disciple of Christ does not mean a renunciation of the world and of one's responsibilities in society. The gesture of the first disciples called by Jesus to leave everything and follow the teacher must be understood in the complexity of the process, in the context of the age and in relation to the special role of the Twelve for the Christian community. Willingness to let go of everything represents the openness and decision of those called to be disciples to reconfigure their lives on completely different coordinates. The focus of the Gospel is on the importance and timeliness of the disciples' response and their changing identity. But as the Gospel shows us, to follow Jesus is to become a person who lives in the world following his model and being ready to carry out his mission. This requires a way of life that is structured around the values of the teacher and implies an effort to participate as partners with God in the process of saving all things. The role of the disciples is to bring meaning and healing to all dimensions of existence and in all the places where they live. Jesus does not call us to leave the world and our responsibilities in society, but invites us to assume them with a new vision and from a new position. Through the message of the Gospel, we have been invited to move from being mere fishermen or goal-oriented people, who have no horizon other than this world, to being fishers of people or disciples who find the meaning of their existence in God's kingdom. The call of the disciples of Jesus draws our attention to the willingness to accept a radical change of life, even if this involves a long and difficult process that we are working on while living in the world. This is how discipleship begins.

Questions

1. To what extent is the current message of the church being conveyed to people as an invitation to become disciples of Jesus Christ?

2. Is membership in a local church the same as being a disciple of the Lord? Explain your answer.

3. Are there special standards or expectations for receiving the identity of a disciple of Jesus?

4. Who would have today the legitimate right to utter the biblical invitation "follow me"?

5. To what extent do you consider that, as a mature Christian, you have a responsibility to be a spiritual mentor and to call others to follow you, to become disciples of Christ?

6. What can we do if the local church we worship in does not emphasize the message of discipleship?

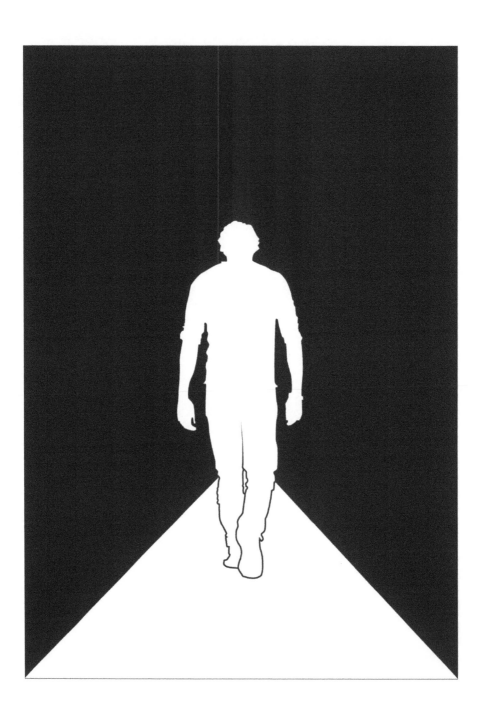

6

Lessons from the Teacher's Mission

We are already familiar with Mark's fast-paced narrative style. In the first three chapters, the disciples witness a succession of tense events, with Jesus as the protagonist, unfolding in Galilee. The scenes are brief and suggest a certain urgency and movement that provoke reactions and manifestations related to the identity and work of an atypical master. Typical forces and characters are immediately mobilized around Jesus: the possessed and the leper, the tax collectors and sinners, the infirm and the sick from the cities, the masses of people and the religious leaders. In the suggested reading framework, the context of these confrontations, with short, dense lessons, represents the school the disciples went through, preparing them for the selection to come (see Mark 3:13–10). If Jesus's strategy was to recruit disciples and prepare them for something specific, then a first stage of this process was to expose them to his own mission, to show them who he is and what he can do. Essentially, the Gospel of Mark outlines three things about Jesus's work: (1) he proclaimed the gospel; (2) he taught people; (3) he healed and cast out demons. The disciples are part of this complex public activity, but somewhat in the background, without them being seen in action or interacting with people and Jesus. They appear as assistants and witnesses to what their teacher is doing, with the freedom to move about in this environment, to ask questions, and to analyse what they see and hear. It is worth highlighting some elements of these scenes focused on the profile of the teacher and his way of working, but also on the possible reactions of the disciples.

First, the master is presented as an authority who in his mission directly confronts all the authorities working in this world. The Gospel highlights the tension and the pressure caused by the figure of Jesus, his authority, and the way he chooses to act. A world of powerlessness and failure flashes before our eyes. The biblical text stresses the human condition (sickness, suffering, decay, bondage), a religious system that no longer works, and the need and expectation of redemption (Mark 1:29–45). It is no accident that the Gospel of Mark places great emphasis in the first chapter on Jesus's healings. They testify to his mission, that he is the servant promised by God to bring salvation to mankind. On the one hand, the biblical text mentions a strong reaction from the world of fallen angels (demons) to the active presence of Jesus (Mark 1:21–28). The constant mention of the unseen reality and its actual presence in people's lives is very suggestive. In apocalyptic style, the biblical author captures the forces of evil at work within creation and its acute need for redemption. The recognition of Jesus's identity by these entities seems surprising and contrasts with the position and dilemmas of humans. The unclean spirits, when they see him, fall to the ground before him and cry out, "You are the Son of God" (Mark 3:11). In Jesus's missionary strategy, his engagement with the unseen world and his exorcisms testify to his identity, to the fact that he is the Son of God and that he has the authority to offer solutions to people's questions and problems. On the other hand, there is a constant confrontation with the Jewish religious leaders who oversee Jesus's work (Mark 2:6–7, 15–17). They are the exponents of an ossified religious system that no longer achieves its goals, they are authorities who have lost their vocation as examples that enhance and energize the lives of believers. The typical reaction of the leaders of the Jewish people shows their concern to maintain their position and influence, and less to recognize the work of God and the need of the people.

The disciples are caught up in this context where a powerful confrontation takes place between Jesus and the authorities that are manifested in this world. To follow Jesus, to be his disciple, implies being able and willing to participate in such a condition, to be at his side in all these confrontations and delimitations. The Gospel underlines the enthusiasm of the masses, the euphoria of those who witness miracles and exorcisms. We can suspect that the disciples were also caught up in this wave of collective exaltation, but we can just as well think that all this had the gift of destabilizing them, of raising questions and fears. In the face of miracles, human beings are vulnerable, their identity and stability are threatened, they are forced to make assessments or decisions. The excitement of the masses who wanted to see signs and wonders may also have animated those invited by Jesus to follow him. But discipleship requires the courage to stand apart from the crowd and refuse to hide comfortably behind others. The teacher's claim demands the emergence from the anonymity of the gregarious being, the flat and conformist spirit that feeds on the impulses of the moment. The crowd readily follows any authority that brings even a small stimulus and can very quickly turn in another direction, to other possible sources that arouse its curiosity and thirst for the extraordinary. We see in Jesus himself a reserve against the enthusiasm of the masses and his strategy of distancing himself from this current because he frequently goes to deserted places to pray and consider his mission (Mark 1:35).

It was important that the first disciples were recruited according to a different paradigm from that offered by the custom of the time, and that Jesus's authority was recognized on the basis of a different kind of relationship with his fellow human beings, not in the logic of crowd psychology. The new teacher imposes himself on the people, on the competition, and above all his opponents, by what he says and does and by the vigour of his identity. For his disciples, it is important that they distinguish him from other possible authorities and eliminate elements of suspicion and mistrust. Jesus calls his disciples to follow him, but this means freely accepting his authority, without rash decisions under the impact of momentary emotions. Even though the biblical text seems to hasten the pace of actions and decisions, the emphasis falls on the importance of a free and lucid response and the timeliness of the offer that comes from God. The teacher calls for a repositioning of their whole life, taking on the implications that flow from this redefinition in relation to their mission and values. This was difficult for Jesus's disciples, and it is difficult for us today. Discipleship begins with this great challenge of accepting an asymmetrical relationship to someone, to a person to whom you give the right to evaluate and define your freedom and whom you obey. It's about a vote of confidence, about the courage to leave your life in the hands of another, about taking risks. In relation to Jesus Christ, Christian identity implies accepting this permanent quality of being a disciple, constantly referring to the authority of the Son of God in all things, assuming the necessity of confronting other authorities to whom it is no longer legitimate to relate through dependence and obedience.

Second, the biblical text draws our attention to the way Jesus related to Jewish tradition and Scripture (Mark 2:18–28). The disciples live in a specific religious, social, and ethical context. They seek solutions to their problems by drawing on what they know and on what the context in which they live offers them. From the master's perspective, an important lesson for the disciples is their ability and willingness to evaluate the standards and values on which they build their lives. The Gospel tells us nothing about the reaction of the disciples when Jesus seems to disregard a number of traditions of the Jewish people or when he confronts the leaders about their hypocritical appropriation of formal religious rules without regard for the spirit of Scripture and the situation of the people. But it is clear that Jesus is making a serious assessment of the elements on which the social and religious experience of the Jewish people at that time was based. Through a few actions, but also through some almost aphoristic formulations, the Gospel of Mark recounts how Jesus brings to light some major issues of understanding and application of Scripture. Correctively, Jesus tells the religious leaders that "those who are well have no need of a physician," "no one puts new wine into old wineskins" or that "the Sabbath was made for man, not man for the Sabbath." The disciples were probably surprised to hear such lines from the teacher, winced at the accusations made by the Pharisees that Jesus was collaborating with the lord of the devils, or were delighted when they were defended (for not fasting or working on the Sabbath). Such experiences and even reversals are part of the discipleship process, and their density is greatest at the beginning of the journey.

Confusion, fear, and mistrust can easily arise in the soul of disciples when what seemed solid and well established under their feet is shaken. In the master's strategy, however, such a process of demolition and rebuilding is essential. What is at stake in discipleship is the shaping of a coherent understanding of the nature of reality and of God, the definition and assumption of a value system that gives a clear identity, a purpose in life, a set of ideals and the path towards them. In general, the disciples lack coherence and the ability to build such an axiological system. They may find that what they know or what they are trying to do generates a crisis and does not provide consistent answers and solutions. They know that they need help, that they are vulnerable, and they are willing to receive help, to learn. We can only suspect such things about the experience of Jesus's disciples at that time. We don't know what triggered their reaction to accept the teacher's call, but the teacher's working strategy shows us their need to have their foundations rebuilt, to reorganize their thinking and their whole life. Discipleship has a cost. Jesus does not spare the disciples from the suffering, dilemmas, confusions, or exaltations of this process. Those who resist and are willing to go all the way share in the benefits of the training, in the results of the experience with the master.

Third, the biblical text highlights something about Jesus's lifestyle and character, his own discipline, his relationship to people and to God. Somehow, we expect the Gospel to give us a glimpse into some of the more intimate details of Jesus's personality. It is part of the seriousness and honesty of the discipleship project that the master is transparent, that he opens up to his disciples and invites them to get to know him. Especially in the beginning phase, it is essential for disciples to be close to the master, to establish a relationship of trust. Even though there is not much material relevant to this discussion in these first three chapters of Mark's Gospel, a few things could be pointed out. It is important to note, to begin with, that Jesus starts his mission at home, in the towns of Galilee. To the disciples, he is a local, probably a familiar but reclusive figure, possibly a bit mysterious. This geographical and social proximity is important. We are not talking about a master from another social class (though there may be such a situation), but a man from the community who has something to offer. The difference in potential is an important key to discipleship. When someone has something to offer and someone else is willing to receive, a mentoring relationship can be established. It is clear that Jesus is a surprise to those in Galilee and to potential disciples. But it seems encouraging to see the prospect of a master rising up from among them, immediately establishing himself as an authority and showing that he can meet the expectations of his followers.

We can also see how the biblical text speaks of a number of features personal to Jesus, albeit discreetly. We see how he is moved by the suffering and misery in which the people of Galilee lived. Jesus shows his compassion for the people, he gets involved in their lives: he enters their homes, he has pity on the sick and the poor, he frees those in bondage to devils and sinful passions. We see the master appreciating people's effort, insistence, faith, and ingenuity (as in the case of those who bring a sick person to him to be healed and lower him into the house through the roof). He is courageous and takes action, even though he knows his opponents' intention to accuse him of not observing all the regulations of a sick religious system (regarding the Sabbath or fasting, for example). The teacher is willing to enter into relationships with people and create the basis for a new kind of human brotherhood, beyond blood ties, on the basis of faith in God and a common value system: "whoever does the will of God, he is my brother and sister and mother" (Mark 3:35). He is a rigorous person and does not give up his own discipline even when he is very much in demand for his mission. He gets up early to make time for prayer and meditation in solitude, he withdraws from the crowd to avoid the excesses of people and the temptation of a false self-image. Last but not least, Jesus rejects the hypocrisy and imposture typical of many religious leaders of the time. Aware of his mission, he does not refuse the company of the marginalized (the poor, sinners, foreigners) or of the social categories denigrated by the religious authorities (tax collectors, the rich).

All these characteristics of Jesus can easily be spotted by the disciples then and today. The authenticity of the master is the basic condition of the disciples' training process. Any form of falsehood and obscurity undermines the dynamics of change and distorts the character of the disciples. The difference in potential available to the teacher must be accompanied by character: honesty, transparency, and generosity. Discipleship is possible when one is ready to open one's life and invest oneself in others for their sake, valuing the freedom and dignity of the disciple with realism and character. Any other data that might lie behind the intention to disciple others will sooner or later lead to failure.

For today's disciples, Jesus's model is accessible both from the Gospel text and from the lives of the disciples who have decided to follow his path and mission. The work of grounding the identity of the disciple of Christ is done in the context of the Christian community. Each generation of new disciples of Jesus must go through the same effort that those called at the beginning went through – as Mark the Evangelist recounts. The role of Christians as disciples of Jesus in the world is to participate effectively in the process of transformation that every person who accepts Christ's authority in his or her life must go through. Continuing the mission of the teacher in the world implies the responsibility to assist others in the dynamics of their becoming. The role of the disciple is in turn to guide others, to support those who wish to follow Jesus Christ. This work is neither easy nor without its challenges. Discipleship of others requires a readiness to make Jesus visible to the person in need of salvation, in need of a life transformation. Disciples of Jesus have been given the authority to continue his mission, but not to replace him in his relationship with those who need him. The use of the authority received from the teacher takes the form of serving the one who wishes to become a disciple, of walking with him the complex path of transformation. It was difficult for the Twelve who were with Jesus in the past, and it is difficult for believers who have decided to follow Christ today. With each generation of people, the process must always be started again because the work of becoming a person and the work of redefining a life that is set in a relationship of discipleship with Jesus Christ cannot be bypassed. The presence of the Son of God with believers in the world is cast in this paradigm of discipleship. The transforming authority of Jesus is visible in his disciples and is accessible to all who wish to follow this path.

Questions

1. What is currently the profile of the evangelical leader who attracts the most people? What characteristics make him/her very attractive and visible?

2. In Christians' assessments of the current culture, which of its characteristics are considered to have the greatest negative impact on their lives and spirituality?

3. What is your understanding of the concept of a mentor?

4. What about that of a prophetic leader?

5. Scripture tells us that Jesus: proclaimed the gospel, taught people, and got involved in their lives, offering them support and solutions. How present are these dimensions in the life of your Christian community?

6. What do you consider to be the Christian values that could bear the most authentic witness to God in the context of today's society?

7. How would you define a nominal Christian or disciple?

7

A First Selection

In the Gospel of Mark, discipleship implies a prompt response from those called by the master to follow him. It also requires that disciples are always with the teacher and participate in his mission. In Christianity, discipleship means following in the footsteps of Jesus; it is the experience of living in his presence. This requires the definition of a new way of life and a new identity resulting from the appropriation of the values, principles, and ideals according to which Jesus Christ lived his life in the world. The Gospel of Mark tells us that people were captivated by the human experience of the Son of God. The miracles he did, the message he spoke, the authority with which he presented himself to the religious leaders of the day attracted a large number of potential disciples. In his characteristic style, the evangelist does not give details of the nature and structure of the extensive group of disciples around Jesus, but he does mention laconically another important episode in the dynamics of discipleship. The scene is briefly recounted in Mark 3 and concerns the selection of a small group of disciples from among those who followed Jesus (Mark 3:13–19). The biblical text creates a sense of entering a new stage in the discipleship process and calls our attention to understanding something of the significance of what happened.

Up to this point, the Gospel of Mark records Jesus issuing a concrete invitation to some people to come and follow him. The biblical text mentions the names of five of the Lord's future disciples, but it suggests that others decided to become disciples and added themselves to the followers of Jesus on their own initiative, convinced of the value and mission of the new teacher from Galilee. We do not know whether Jesus is following a custom of the time or has a well-defined strategy, but after a period of action he decides to make a selection of those who will follow him. Without giving any information about selection criteria and without mentioning any possible tests to which potential disciples were subjected, Mark the Evangelist notes that Jesus went up a mountain and called to him a group of disciples from the crowd of people who were following him. The text suggests that there was a clear intention on Jesus's part to choose this group and work more closely with them. From the great mass of admirers, the master invited to the meeting on the mountain whomever he wished or considered appropriate. Those selected responded and followed the master, probably without knowing exactly what was next. This scene of the climbing of the mountain contrasts with the previous one, where the biblical passage tells us that a crowd of people (from Galilee, Judea, Jerusalem, Tyre, Sidon, etc.) came to see Jesus. The retreat from the crowd, together with the ascent of the mountain, seems to suggest an initiatory experience, a gesture that implies the passage to a new stage in the formation process. The scene itself brings to mind many similar examples from the Old Testament, in which the mountain is presented as a preferred place of human encounter with God, a select but uncomfortable, tense space, a place where the one who has ventured to climb is put to the test.

In the Gospel picture we consider here, the context suggests ascent and evaluation in the context of discipleship. Like the patriarchs of old, the disciples are required to distance themselves from events, from the reactions of the masses of people, from the confusion created by miracles and exorcisms, from the routine of daily concerns. Once the disciples have had the opportunity to better discover the personality and mission of the teacher, once the stakes of following him become clearer (as evidenced by the confrontation with the authorities or by the challenge of re-evaluating one's own identity and spiritual traditions), the need to take a further step is emerging. After a period of settling in and testing, an evaluation takes place: the master evaluates those who have enrolled to be his disciples and makes a decision on who enters the next stage. The biblical text does not explain the meaning of this selection that Jesus makes, but we intuit that it is an evaluation of the candidates and what has been achieved up to this point.

The need for evaluation derives from the very nature of the discipleship process. It requires a commitment from both parties, master and disciple alike, and launches a process based on mutual trust, freedom, and the affirmation of each person's dignity. These essential dimensions cannot be taken for granted in the discipleship relationship. There are possible risks, dangers, abuses, and forms of failure inherent in such a human experience. Even for the most well-intentioned there can be critical moments, reformulations of expectations, and reassessments of goals. In Christian discipleship even the master can have his moments of weakness and temptations about deviating from the essence of the assumed mission. The adventure of discipleship is an experience that requires continuous evaluation. Both master and apprentice have the right and the responsibility to analyze things: oneself and the other; the dynamics of the relationship; the results of the process of becoming; the strategy; and the goals set. Discernment and evaluation are needed for the health of the discipleship process, in order to remove the dangers and let the assumed core values work. Especially in the early stages, testing is an essential ingredient of apprenticeship. On these evaluative occasions, those who have rushed in and misunderstood what discipleship entails can step back or reaffirm their commitment by being willing to better understand and correct what is missing. The master also has the opportunity to confirm or refute the disciples' journey in relation to what was initially agreed upon. The master's evaluation may involve defining categories of disciples, outlining differences in potential and action, and defining different working strategies for each individual or for groups of disciples. In turn, the disciple can sense how things work, whether the relationship with the master produces becoming and whether their relationship is built on the values established at the beginning of the process.

Mark reveals that Jesus's selection takes place on two levels. The first corresponds to the invitation to go up the mountain. The master thus chooses, decides, and recognizes those who will follow him in his further adventure (Mark 3:13). Those who are now called go beyond the stage of mere admirers, beyond the status of individuals driven by superficial interests. They understand that following Jesus is more than just benefiting from miracles and signs, or a provisional status as a member of a group that sympathizes with a young rabbi. Because they have been invited, we can understand that something much deeper has happened in their being, that they have passed a basic test and have gone beyond the sentimental and basic level of following Jesus. They have received the teacher's confirmation and become members of a new community, with a new status that generates a different kind of solidarity. These are the validated disciples of Jesus. In this initiatory setting, in the discrete gathering on that mountain, we can understand that the Gospel of Mark outlines the idea of establishing a foundation for the future of the church. The new community of Jesus is built on the foundation of discipleship. Of the many called, few are chosen. It is not enough to be called. One must accept the invitation and follow the way of the master. This path is not easy and cannot be pursued out of inertia. It is an ascent that defines and carves out a new identity, and the journey involves tests and evaluations that confirm the quality of a genuine disciple. There are no such things as nominal disciples, and you cannot declare yourself a disciple of Jesus without validation of this status. Discipleship is not about people assuming a label and a formal name, a convenient contextual positioning because it is demanded by a trend or because it brings effortless benefits. The selection made by the master inevitably indicates exigency, seriousness, and the willingness to assume the condition of the master. It is not a coincidence that after the selection of the disciples, Mark presents a terrible confrontation of Jesus with the leaders of Jerusalem (Mark 3:20–30), on which occasion the new teacher is accused of being mad and working with Beelzebul (the lord of the devils). The choice of disciples takes place at a time when it is uncomfortable for them to be associated with Jesus, a time when the teacher's identity is questioned by the leaders of society, and serious accusations are made against him. To stay on his side requires a certain degree of knowledge, confidence, strength of character, and courage. To agree to follow him and climb the mountain you need something that makes you like the master, the willingness and readiness to be one with him.

The second level of selection operated by Jesus takes place on the mountain itself, among the disciples already confirmed. The biblical text tells us that the teacher chose twelve of his disciples to have with him and to send them out to proclaim the gospel (Mark 3:14–19). Before further commenting on this scene, it is important to look at the community building around Jesus on the basis of discipleship. In the biblical context, this small group established by Jesus appeals to the symbolism of the chosen people and the twelve tribes of Israel. If we accept this parallelism (rooted in the prophets and the wisdom books), then Jesus's gesture of selecting a small group of disciples from the others signals the establishment of a foundation for God's new community in the world, the church. The Jewish people was built on the twelve sons of Jacob; the church is built on the twelve apostles chosen by Jesus. Israel has an ethnic, blood constitution; Jesus's community is built on the value of discipleship. The Jewish people defines its identity by the law of God received at Sinai; the new Israel is built on the good news brought by Jesus Christ and on what he has achieved as a man in the world.

Returning to what the Gospel text emphasizes about the election of the Twelve, several important elements can be observed. First, Mark shows us that Jesus's choice points to a new stage in the discipleship process. The teacher redefines the status of disciples from those who follow him to those who are with him. The new stage of discipleship involves being with Jesus, identifying with him and his mission. The disciples' participation in the master's condition suggests a closeness and a type of relationship that has advanced from the period of the first trials and searches. It is the stage in which the work of formation, the process of Jesus's investiture in his disciples, takes on a new dimension. Second, the biblical text underlines the missionary dimension of the choice of the Twelve. Jesus entrusts the disciples with his own mission. On their shoulders rests the responsibility for the continuity of the master's work in the world. This is where discipleship finds its full meaning: the disciple is called to become like his master, to be ready to carry forward his vision and mission and to be able to prepare others to do the same. Third, the biblical text mentions that Jesus gave the disciples the authority to heal and cast out demons (Mark 3:15). This empowerment is the result of the discipleship process. The true authority of the teacher is confirmed by the disciples' development, transforming their being and shaping a personality that puts into action what has been developed through the relationship with the teacher. By its nature, discipleship is a growth process in the context of authority. The master uses his authority to enhance the being of the apprentices, to lead them towards maturity and fulfilment. The teacher also gives authority to the disciples, allowing them space and freedom of expression to shape them as future disciple makers, who are able to invest themselves in others. With these brief mentions Mark 3 outlines the future path of the disciples' adventure with Jesus. We will identify some of the details of this journey as we continue reading the following chapters of the Gospel.

The experience that Jesus's contemporary disciples went through is still valid today. The new identity and the coherent placement on the path of discipleship are not without dilemmas, trials, lessons, and examinations. The journey from being an admirer of Jesus or of his values to assuming and clearly validating discipleship is not the same for everyone, but it is not without the exercise of confronting oneself and making choices. Leaving the confines of an old way of life and accepting the demands of discipleship under the authority of Christ involves many moments and stages of evaluation and confirmation. Sometimes we can benefit from selection frameworks like the one on the mountain, through particular people and circumstances. At other times things are clarified momentarily and on a personal level through decisions and the setting of demarcation lines.

Associating with Jesus is a challenge for all time. The tests of discipleship are frequently given in this area of our ability to remain faithful to the master, not to betray him in the face of the challenges of the world, and not to give up our assumed identity. Jesus's promises, that he remains with us until the end of history and that he is with each generation of disciples to support them in bearing the burdens and responsibilities assumed, are constantly renewed and fulfilled in the lives of believers. This is most clearly visible in the more mature disciples, those who have already travelled a good part of the way with Christ. The tests of discipleship are not meant to reveal how good we are, but how authentic our choices and lives are. They always show that the teacher is with us and that his disciples are in solidarity and have a better understanding of the task of serving their brothers.

Questions

1. What aspects make us vulnerable in our relationships today, especially in terms of faithfulness to God and to our mentors?

2. If Jesus desires the salvation of human beings, is he not too demanding in terms of the standards he asks of us as we seek to become his disciples? How might we resolve this tension?

3. To what extent can we trust people, both ordinary Christians and those who serve as mentors?

4. Should the church be more elitist and assertive in terms of gospel values? Why and in what respect?

5. In your desire to become a disciple, have you ever been turned down by a potential mentors? How did you handle that situation?

6. Have you ever been put in the situation of refusing someone who wanted to become your disciple? What were the reasons for that refusal?

8

Being Close to the Master

We have seen that discipleship enters another stage after a selection process and the master's decision to identify working groups and goals for what follows. After the disciples have had the opportunity to hear and see the master from a distance, the prospect of being with him in private is now open to them, and the focus of the relationship changes. Chapters 4 and 5 of Mark's Gospel reveal that Jesus begins to focus his attention on the work of teaching the disciples. The biblical text also highlights something about his working strategy. On the one hand, the disciples receive the teaching publicly, along with all those who come to listen to Jesus. The teacher presents his ideas in a way that is typical in the Jewish tradition – he tells parables or conveys certain ideas with the help of stories with a twist. On the other hand, the disciples are given a special time of dialogue, and they receive explanations of what they have heard, with the opportunity to ask questions and receive clarification (see Mark 4:10, 34). Jesus takes the initiative in these small group dialogues when he sees the disciples puzzled or scandalized by what they have heard, and sometimes when he wants to evaluate what they have understood. At the same time, it should be emphasized that the Gospel records that Jesus continues his mission and that the disciples assist him and participate in all his actions: proclamations, healings and miracles, and confrontations with various categories of people. It is clear that, for Jesus, discipleship is not the purpose of his activity, but a way of preparing servants capable of taking up his mission and carrying it forward. The work of formation takes place both through exposure to Christ's teaching, in public and in private, and through actual participation in his actions. The biblical text captures some nuances of the formative process after the selection of disciples and their commitment to follow Jesus in all he does.

We can first ask why Jesus spoke to people in parables (Mark 4:1–34), and what impact this method had on discipleship. Chapter 4 of the Gospel suggests some possible answers. On the one hand, we see that this kind of presentation of his teaching raises questions among the listeners. Jesus stimulates the interrogative dimension and puts the disciples to work. The act of learning is not a comfortable one. It requires an effort to open one's being to what the teacher is saying, a work of evaluation, and a receptive readiness to the content transmitted. It is not a question of whether or not the disciples have understood a particular message, because parabolic discourse is one that lends itself to multiple meanings and very diverse connections. What is essential is that whatever the disciples have grasped is discussed with the teacher. Without this possibility of debate and evaluation, of questioning and reacting, there is no genuine discipleship. In intimacy with the master, disciples can formulate their ideas, questions, and puzzles and receive answers or clarifying questions. Although the passage in Mark 4:11–12 is complex and difficult to interpret, in the context of discipleship, this text seems to emphasize a relatively simple truth: people cannot understand biblical revelation, the meaning of the presence in the world of the Son of God unless they are willing to become disciples of Jesus, to sit in his presence and receive answers to their fundamental questions.

Discipleship thus appears as a gift to people, a setting in which knowledge of God becomes accessible to human experience. Disciples are given an understanding of Jesus's message because they have committed themselves to follow him unconditionally, to be with him and to accept the uncomfortable process of transformation that leads to knowledge. On the other hand, through the parables, a revelatory and prophetic mechanism can be triggered in listeners. Jesus uses familiar parables or themes from the Jewish tradition, but adds a personal emphasis to them, sometimes with slight nuances, sometimes with more profound changes. But by appealing to a context with which the listener is familiar, the parable can give a chance for a glimpse, a chance for an understanding or evaluation of what is considered familiar. By using parables, Jesus frequently refers to truths presented in the Old Testament, to lessons from the history of the chosen people, and to divine promises yet to be fulfilled. Their evaluative and critical function, but especially their clarifying function, is frequently seen in the reactions of people and in the attitudes of leaders who understand the message of the parables and grasp the meaning of what Jesus says. The same reaction mechanism can be seen in the disciples. Jesus's parables challenge them, help them to revisit elements assimilated from tradition without a critical effort of distillation, and enable them to re-examine things in a new light. Jesus's pedagogy is exemplary. It does not spare any effort and it does not suppress the freedom of questioning and decision-making. The master is at the disciple's disposal as one who produces especially good questions, but not gratuitous and convenient answers. He cannot hide confrontations, critical analyses, and doubts, but he can undermine cheap certainties and easy placement in the commonplaces of knowledge.

We need to understand what the master was trying to achieve by applying such an interesting strategy as that of using parables. Mark seems to help us understand the stakes of the formative exercise to which the disciples are subjected. In Mark 4, he presents three short texts on the subject of the light of knowledge and the process of human change under its action (Mark 4:1–20, 26–29, 30–34). Like the others around, the disciples experience their own forms of blindness and darkness. The presence of the master is for them a source of light with a transformative potential. But receiving the light of understanding is not easy for the disciples. The teaching they receive brings a strong confrontation with the self: hidden things, self-limitations, collapsing meanings, doubts about their own identity. The tension created is about willingness to accept change and responsibility for the truth received. Discipleship is nothing like attending a conference where one can hear a delightful or interesting speech and then easily forget it. The disciples, once exposed to the master's teaching, go through the uncomfortable mechanism of their own transformation, and become themselves agents of the light of knowledge of which they were made partakers. The purpose of light is to dispel darkness, both the darkness within and the darkness of the disciple's daily life. Those who wish to be disciples must be able to take the risk of being consumed themselves by the fire of knowledge and to carry this "virus" with them in all the details of their life. In a sense, discipleship is a road of no return. Those who submitted to exposing themselves to the light can no longer live as if they are in darkness, can no longer justify their own actions under the cover of ignorance, can no longer remain indifferent to what happens to them and to those around them. Although there is the risk of failure (either burning one's wings like Icarus if you soar too high, or losing all one has like Judas, if one uses the gifts received for other purposes), those who stood by the teacher carry the burden and gift of knowledge and can no longer deny it. The right path of discipleship is the transformation of one's being and the building of a new identity, like the seed sown in good soil that sprouts, grows, and bears fruit. The two small parables in Mark 4 underline the dynamics of discipleship, the power of truth to bring about change, the optimistic outlook of the process despite the inherent difficulties and risks.

In the context of Christian spirituality, the guarantor of this process of human transformation is God himself. His kingdom develops on these foundations which take into account the nature of human beings and their destiny, which is linked to their knowledge of the truth. Humans are ever-changing beings, and their identity involves transformation. The specific nature of the process calls for acceptance of mentoring relationships, a willingness to follow in the footsteps of someone who knows the way, and to take on the demands of being an apprentice. What Jesus achieved with his disciples is the standard, not the exception, of the Christian life. Whoever wants to be a Christian must agree to be a disciple of Jesus. Likewise, those who have already travelled a part of the road to maturity have to show the way to those who are seeking it or who are at the beginning of the climb.

It should also be noted that in Jesus's strategy of training the disciples, he exposes them to experiences that highlight the qualities of some of the people who surprise Jesus with their faith and courage. In Mark 5, there are two miracles that Jesus performs, concerning the faith of a sick woman (Mark 5:21–34) and a synagogue leader (Mark 5:35–43). At least two aspects are relevant to the theme of discipleship here. On the one hand, disciples must learn that an important dimension of God's economy demands human faith. Disciples can only be people of faith, animated by a strong faith that is sustained by a depth of dependence on God and an understanding that only he can provide the solutions we need. On the other hand, the disciples have the opportunity to learn from Jesus how people's faith works and how the teacher responds to it. Both cases point to people who are able to transcend their condition, and to do things they would not normally do. We are also dealing with two determined people, convinced that Jesus can fulfil their desire, that he can respond to their need, and that he is the only solution. Although neither Jesus nor the biblical author say anything about whether or not the two would have become disciples of Jesus, it is clear that they are good examples of the disciple from afar, the believer who saw in Jesus God's solution for people.

Finally, we note that for the master, discipleship is not an end in itself. The teacher is not merely a disciple-maker, someone who teaches a subject to a group of pupils, and when he has completed the cycle of lessons, he starts the process again with others. On the contrary, disciples are invited to take part in a training process in the context of a mission, of an activity undertaken by the teacher. Discipleship is a special kind of school. Those involved have to learn, to acquire some knowledge, but the process involves on-the-job training. It involves someone who is trained in the field and puts a set of skills to work, and the apprentices are involved in the story, they become part of the action with their teacher. It is only in the context of taking on the teacher's mission and strategy that disciples begin to learn their vocation. We notice that Jesus did not take a break from his work in order to train a group of disciples. Despite the fact that he very quickly became uncomfortable for the leaders of the Jewish people and the Roman authorities, he asked his disciples to follow him, to be part of what he was doing and to fully assume the conditions of his mission. Exposing the disciples to the concrete work of the master is the best opportunity to get to know and build trust in relationships. The teacher puts his whole being to work in the actions of his mission and becomes accessible to the questioning and critical eye of the disciples. Jesus's ever fresh and frequently challenging personality strengthened the disciples' confidence and decision to follow him even when they failed to understand the logic of what he said or the meaning of his actions. At the same time, however, the presence of the disciples with Jesus in action provided the gift of testing, of shaking that trust. Frequently, the disciples also ask the questions that are on the lips of the crowd about Jesus's identity. Often they have doubts about the choice they have made and realize that association with their teacher is uncomfortable, even risky. Discipleship is not exempt from these impediments, and its reality is clear from the experience of the Twelve with Jesus. But the results of the process build the strength and courage to go on, to benefit from the results of becoming. In discipleship, no illusions are sold, either about the difficulties and realism of the road ahead or about what can be achieved. Everything is built step by step, with rigour and in action, with risks and stumbles, with the empowering assistance of the teacher who triggers the most unexpected leaps in apprentices so that they can always overcome their condition.

Perhaps the most complex question that those who want to be disciples of Jesus can ask today is about the meaning of the teacher's mission and the possibility of actualizing it in the present. We can glimpse something of the essence of this mission if we look at Christ with the critical eye of the Jew who saw him at work then. Jesus assumed the role of prophet and scholar, a role with very clear characteristics in the Jewish community. His function was a complex one, responding to needs that today are covered by several professions in the context of modern society (teacher, doctor, lawyer, clergyman). Jesus fulfils these functions and does so from a new position, bringing with it meaning and clarification about the plan of God, the role of human beings in the world, and the divine invitation to a fundamental change of thinking and behaviour in order to live life in accordance with God's economy in history. To be disciples is to actualize the mission of Jesus in the world. This is the meaning of the idea of being salt and light where we have been placed, of living our lives and fulfilling our responsibilities as people who have accepted the truth of the revelation brought by Jesus Christ and who thus participate with him in the great work of salvation of the whole world. Discipleship involves assuming a new identity and a life lived according to the values promoted by Jesus, a readiness to serve others in a wide variety of ways and thus to prove that the kingdom of God is real and has come to people. In fulfilling their mission, Jesus's disciples become witnesses and enable others to believe, to question and search for meaning, to understand God's call and what he offers through the incarnation of his Son. As we have already seen, such a mission is a lifelong one. The disciples start from the bottom, from the foundations, demolish some things that are inadequate and build in their place other things that are lasting, accept the truths of Christ and allow themselves to be permanently transformed by them, assimilating values, acquiring experiences – all of which result in maturity and can be converted into elements that can be communicated to others.

Questions

1. How much transparency and closeness can be achieved between a disciple and a mentor in the contemporary church? What are the most important obstacles in this direction?

2. How can Christian discipleship be transformed from a way of life and a means towards maturity into an end in itself?

3. What are the most uncomfortable aspects of discipleship from the perspective of today's Christian?

4. How would you evaluate your discipleship with Jesus? What are the aspects in which you consider yourself most deficient? What about the ones in which you feel most satisfied?

5. Are there dimensions of Jesus's personality that make him more accessible to people today than in the past? What would these be and how would they function relationally?

9

Disciples Put into Practice

As we progress through the Gospel of Mark, we notice that the master and the disciples have gone deep into the training process. On the one hand, things are unfolding in the pattern of ancient times and Jewish tradition. Jesus is always accompanied by the disciples in his work and thus offers them the possibility of transformation through direct interaction, observation, asking questions, etc. On the other hand, the teacher involves the disciples in confrontations with the religious and political leaders of Israel, in the problems of the people who come to Jesus for solutions, and in the tension arising from the resistance of the unseen world of the fallen angels. This harsh school does not spare Christ-followers, but constantly tests their faith, their convictions, and their character. The tension curve of discipleship reaches ever higher levels. After a period of intense lessons, we expect to see the next step and possibly what triggers entry into a new stage of discipleship. Chapter 6 of the Gospel of Mark tells us that the Saviour decides to go to his native land (the land of Galilee, Nazareth) to do what he usually did there: preach the gospel, teach people, heal the sick, and release from their bondage those possessed by demons. The biblical text says that the locals do not welcome him and question his mission. The main objection is to Jesus's identity: how can a carpenter's son (who probably learned his father's crafts and was an apprentice in his workplace) assume such a position as teacher or rabbi? By what power does he work miracles? Where does he get the wisdom that intrigues them? The conclusion of the biblical author is that Jesus was unable to fulfil his mission there, that he had an unbelieving, even hostile audience and decided to leave for other destinations.

In this interesting setting, where Jesus is rejected by his countrymen – and possibly by his family – he decides to send his disciples to put into practice the things they have seen and heard from him (Mark 6:7–13). We might ask: why now? Is the master going through a crisis because he is rejected at home and wants to see if he is accepted elsewhere? Or is this a good time for the disciples to act and assess the consistency of their identity at a time that seems complicated for the mission? Regardless of the answer, it is clear that we are at an important point in the discipleship process. This also seems to be suggested by the logic of the biblical text. At this point, Mark, almost as never before, becomes meticulous and attentive to detail, carefully, even with finesse, presenting some aspects of the discipleship period. This is reason enough for us to take a special interest in these elements that reveal the importance of the stage reached in the discipleship process.

A first detail emphasized by Scripture is that of sending. As the teacher's envoys, the disciples are given the responsibility to carry forward his specific project. Jesus has commissioned the disciples with his special mission and thus defines their quality as disciples through this fundamental coordinate of the continuity of the work he is doing. On this occasion of being sent into ministry, the main objective of discipleship is also reaffirmed: the formation of persons capable of carrying on a ministry, a tradition, a system of values, a way of life. In order to assess the disciples' ability to ensure the continuity of the master's mission, they will be put to the practical test, and given the opportunity to put into action what they have seen and heard. This practical dimension of discipleship is the context in which both the disciples and the master are subjected to a concrete evaluation in relation to the purpose of their mission in the world. If the disciples are not able to do what the teacher asks of them, it means that something has not worked well so far, that something has broken along the way, or that something should be reassessed. However, as the apprenticeship process is not finished, this practical stage is not only an opportunity to evaluate, but also a chance to make some corrections and overcome some limitations, to assume mistakes and point out deficiencies.

The biblical text also states that they were sent out two by two (Mark 6:7). Perhaps one explanation for this approach can be linked to the Jewish custom of requiring at least two witnesses to support a testimony. Another interpretation would take into account the realism of the action, because the disciples are sent on a journey with many risks (the journey between the villages and cities of Galilee was not a walk in the park). But we might as well consider this sending out in groups of two as another lesson in discipleship. This process is not only about the disciple-teacher relationship, but also about the relationship between the disciples. Jesus worked with a group and built a community vision different from the traditional one. The community of Christ's followers is based on a type of brotherhood that is not based on unity of blood, ethnicity, race, or religion, but on the assumption of the same identity as disciples of the Lord (see Mark 3:35). Team spirit, the ability to work together with someone (who is different in thought and action), and the willingness to depend on the other are important qualities that are developed in the discipleship process.

Another important aspect of the sending of the disciples is captured in a textual formula that is not easy to understand: giving them "authority over the unclean spirits" (Mark 6:7). Without going into hermeneutical detail, the text seems to suggest that we are dealing with a transfer or delegation of authority from the master to the disciples. By its nature, authority implies this logic of continuity, of receiving and passing it on. The teacher is one who produces development in the disciples – he facilitates a transformation that enhances their being and makes them capable of fulfilling the teacher's mission. In discipleship, however, even the master is required to prove himself as an authority. He does this in various forms, and in this case he shows that he, in turn, is an envoy who has received authority, is an investment of another. The Gospel repeats on numerous occasions that Jesus assumed this quality of being sent by the Father, that he always worked under the Father's authority and therefore always had God's assistance and guidance in everything he did. The idea of empowering the disciples does not necessarily imply ceremony and symbolic gestures (although it may include such actions). It is an investment of trust in what has already been built up in them through their relationship with the master; a confirmation that the teacher gives the disciples, that they are ready for action; a presence that assists them on their journey and confirms that they are on the right path; an assistance of the Holy Spirit who has always worked in Christ's life as well. The mention of authority over unclean spirits clearly leads to the core of Christ's restorative economy, which sets all things back into their normal relationship with God and brings them out from under the bondage of the evil one. As disciples of Jesus they become exponents of the work of salvation and liberation, co-participants in God's work in the world.

It is particularly interesting that the disciples were asked to depend only on what they had received from their teacher and nothing else. They were not even to depend on the means of subsistence (Mark 6:8–9). The biblical text tells us that Jesus commanded the disciples to take nothing with them on the journey: no bread, no money, no purse. It was suggested that they take only one set of clothes, sandals (a vital item of clothing for travelling long distances, probably on foot, but also a symbol of being prepared) and a staff (an instrument of support and protection, but also a sign of sending and authority). Perhaps as we interpret the message Jesus is giving here we should take into consideration both the practical dimension of sending and the paradigmatic dimension of imitating the master. A journey requires preparation and resources – costly logistics that can facilitate, impede, or even derail its purpose. The disciples must be prepared for the mission, but the emphasis falls on an articulate and ready personal profile, consistency of character, and the instruction received from the teacher. At the same time, the master asks the disciples to put their faith to work and to focus solely on their mission, trusting that God is looking after them. It is essential that the disciples be obedient, trust the teacher's word, and put into practice what they are asked to do, despite their worries and concerns (from basic needs to possible risks and dangers). The radicalism of Jesus's demands as he sends out the disciples may be shocking to the contemporary reader who would insist on considerably more detail when organizing a missionary journey. But Jesus wants to emphasize what is essential, namely the consistency of the disciple's identity and his or her faith, not his or her managerial skills.

An important element of equipping disciples for mission is discernment, the ability to understand the quality of the audience, and the receptivity and openness of people to their message and action (Mark 6:10–11). As a strategy, Jesus asks the disciples to identify good hosts, people of character who are willing to support their mission. That is why he recommends that they enter such homes and stay there while they are in the cities they visit. Let's not forget that this was the pattern Jesus followed. He used to enter people's homes, sit with them at the table, listen to their needs, and give them a message or heal them. With this strategy, Jesus identified and recruited his disciples. The continuation of the master's mission involves using strategies learned from him, and above all taking care to make other disciples. Authentic disciples tend to be like their master, that is, to become themselves disciple-makers. Fulfilling the teacher's mandate of being messengers involves identifying potential disciples and being concerned to pass on to others the treasure received from Jesus. It is an investment (however small, depending on how long the disciples were to stay in a city) that weighs heavily on both sides. The one sent now had the opportunity to be the giver, and the potential apprentice had the chance to see the results of the discipleship process at work. The strategy of going into people's homes is not just specific to ancient Jewish culture, but an important dimension of Christian spirituality learned from our master Jesus Christ. This aspect shows us that discipleship is about our life in its totality, not just an intellectual level of instruction that could easily be institutionalized as courses or lessons in well-defined formal settings. Entering into people's homes is equivalent to taking part in their lives, with all their aspects, and showing people that Christian discipleship offers the framework to understand anew all the facts of our lives.

The biblical text also emphasizes that if Jesus's disciples are not received with openness in some place, it is good not to get into disputes or conflicts, but to leave. This message is prophetic and also functions as a warning. On the one hand, following Jesus presupposes human freedom, the conviction that what is offered is valuable and leads to commitment. There is no discipleship if one eludes this fundamental basis of one's free decision to follow a teacher. There can be no progress in discipleship if the freedom of the disciple is reduced or taken away. On the contrary, in the process, the disciple is led to even greater freedom. On the other hand, the biblical text invites us to be realistic. Jesus himself was rejected by his own people, by his own city and by people of his own ethnicity and religion. Jesus warns the genuine disciples that they can have no other welcome in the world but will share the same condition as the master.

Mark's conclusion to this section (Mark 6:12–13) is brief and points out that the disciples went out and did what Jesus asked of them: they preached repentance, cast out demons, and healed people after anointing with oil. In other words, things worked. The teacher did his job well, and the disciples obeyed the teacher and did what he asked. This result is a testimony that the disciples' lives have changed, that their transformation is real, and they have advanced in the process of training with the teacher. The Gospel of Mark does not discuss any evaluation of the results of the practical test after the disciples' return from action. In Mark 6:30 there is only a brief mention of the return of the Twelve, namely that they told Jesus all that they had done and taught the people. Even with this brief mention, there are indications that evaluation is part of the discipleship process and is important. It must be done systematically, at every stage, and with the utmost seriousness. It is essential that the disciples analyse the results of their work and the concrete results of the mission, but much more important is to see how these have led to the development of their being. But let us not forget that the apprenticeship is not over after the first practical test, whether it is a victory or a failure.

Sending out disciples is not only part of the discipleship process, but also an action that has a paradigmatic function for the Christian community. The Twelve are given the authority to go out into the world to continue the work of Jesus, and they are already participating in this mission before their separation from the teacher. For the disciples, this exercise is edifying and demonstrates the effectiveness of God's economy in the world. It already sets them in the framework in which they will live and act after they reach sufficient maturity, and the master sends them out into the world again. The continuation of Jesus's mission relies on both the effective presence of divine authority in history, and that the disciples assume this authority and put it to work. It is to this partnership that the biblical text seems to draw our attention.

Discipleship in our day does not necessarily have to do with such distinct stages as the sending of disciples to parts of Israel in the past. But as disciples of Christ, we are invited to learn and to put into practice what we have received from the master. Even though we sometimes have the opportunity for phases or periods more clearly focused on preparation and accumulation, this does not happen in isolation without being required to live our lives and to put to work what we receive. Likewise, even if we have already come a long way and have begun to invest in others and make disciples, it does not mean that the work of training is over. Our whole life lived in this world is under the paradigm of discipleship, that is, of an ongoing process of formation and transformation, and at the same time of a way of life that fulfils the mission of Christ in concrete historical contexts.

Questions

1. What do today's mentors lack that does not allow them to encourage their disciples to follow their model of life to a greater extent?

2. How can we imitate Christ today, and how could we use his authority as his disciples?

3. If we are not actively participating in Jesus's mission to the world, is it because we think we are unprepared or because we do not have sufficient authority?

4. How can we avoid the risk of becoming mere clones, through imitation of our mentors in Christian churches?

5. Analyse a moment of crisis from your own discipleship experience (either as a mentor or as a disciple). How much did your trust in the other person matter in resolving that crisis?

10

The Work of Formation Continues

Disciples were sent to put into practice what they saw Jesus doing, because discipleship is not an end in itself, but a process of formation, a work of preparation for a mission, and participation in that mission. This stage of implementation does not come after a long effort of accumulation of knowledge, or preparation through exposure to lessons and theoretical learning. Direct confrontation with the reality for which people are being formed plays a very important role in correctly assessing the preparation state of the disciples, the specific needs of each one, the questions and gaps that need to be filled in the future, etc. As a strategy, Jesus combined the exposition of teaching with the concrete involvement of the disciples in his mission, including periods when he left them to act on their own. The formation of the disciples took place constantly in the context of the teacher's mission; it was not an independent, collateral project. It had the concrete context of the master's engagement in actions, conversations, and speeches, in tests and traps set by opponents, and in periods of rest and withdrawal from the public space.

Perhaps the most intriguing thing about Jesus's teaching and ministry was the way he related to the Scriptures and the traditions of the Jewish people (Mark 7:1–23). The teacher sometimes decides to challenge the minds and understanding of the people or of the religious leaders, and sometimes he is himself confronted by the teachers of the law on certain sensitive topics in his mission. The disciples witness these moments when Jesus is asked to explain and become themselves part of a process of evaluating what they know, what they have learned from tradition, and how they behave based on this heritage. We are going to look at some of the ways in which the master builds solid teaching and character structures in his disciples. Mark is not very generous in this respect, but, apart from the few discourses, we can discern from the development of the narratives a number of important elements for the disciples' formation process.

One of Jesus's few sermons in this Gospel appears in Mark 7 and deals with the traditions of the Jewish people. The context is an observation by the teachers of the law, Pharisees, and scribes, that Jesus's disciples ate without washing their hands (Mark 7:1–13). It is striking in Mark that, before actually presenting the confrontation between Jesus and these officials of the religious system, he insists on presenting a set of rules given as examples from Jewish tradition that people are obliged to follow. We take this parenthesis of the biblical text as a clue to the importance or the seriousness of the subject under discussion. The religious leaders blame the disciples, and the teacher is called to account as to why they do not respect the ancestral tradition. Jesus's response is lengthy and comes in two stages, the first involving the Pharisees and the second the disciples.

In the first stage, Jesus publicly expresses what he believes on the subject raised by the Pharisees. The speech is an elaborate one and contains an argument that is important for the training of the disciples and can be followed in three steps.

First, the teacher does not challenge the concept of tradition or the idea of respect for it. On the contrary, he seems to draw attention to two types of traditions that can develop in the context of a community's history. One is that which takes up and carries forward the fundamentals without altering them, but uses them for a healthy dynamic of believers. The identity of the Jewish people is built on the Scriptures, on the word of God handed down from one generation to the next, as the foundation of the existence of each individual and of society as a whole. This is the source for answering the questions and issues raised by community life and its place in God's plan. In this sense, tradition is precisely the actualization and concretization of divine law in each generation in a complex of elements such as symbols, values, practices, and beliefs that give content and continuity to a particular identity. The second variety of development is that in which, for various reasons, the elements constituting tradition are no longer based on the foundations received from God but on human rules and precepts. If things evolve in this way, then identity is diluted and receives new coordinates, far from what was expected, and far from what would be built by preserving the core that founded the community. From the perspective of discipleship, the discussion outlines the wider context in which discipleship takes place. Everything unfolds in this complex matrix of the mechanism of receiving and passing on a value system.

An authentic master helps the disciple to understand this system and warns him of potential dangers.

Second, Jesus appeals to the texts of the prophets who warn of the danger of the distortion of tradition and the need to have an alert mind and discernment of the times. The school of discipleship is not about breaking out of the mould of community tradition or developing one in parallel, but about experiencing it from a critical perspective. The role of the teacher is to develop in disciples this capacity to evaluate things, and to update and use the prophetic spirit in their formation process. Jesus's reference to the Scriptures is part of this formative effort to develop a sense for authenticity and value and the courage to expose imposture. In the text quoted from Isaiah, the focus is on the lack of character, the lies and falsehood in which people and their leaders live when the law of God has become a mere screen for petty interests. When tradition focuses on the transmission of empty forms without any concrete function, the identity of the people is threatened, and the effects are not long in coming. The scholar points out that any community experience needs an assumed axiological and spiritual context and that it cannot be achieved in a vacuum. If one value system transmitted from the founding fathers is abandoned, another will certainly take its place. If God's law is forgotten, another law will be found to replace it. The same applies to the process of formation, and therefore also to discipleship. Jesus tries to help his disciples understand these things and points out that there is a danger of false discipleship. Tradition is about passing on a way of life, and forming a new generation of leaders, that is, applying discipleship as a core value. The seriousness and quality of the process depend not only on the rigour of the school, but also on the content transmitted. Jesus confronts the religious leaders of the time in their double capacity: on the one hand, as people formed in a corrupt system, with a weak value system, with rules and principles that have abdicated from the truths of Scripture; on the other hand, as authorities who perpetuate the degenerate things of the past, who continue the falsehood and hypocrisy, group interests, and the facade of religiosity.

Third, the master exemplifies a case and shows the mechanism by which a change of perspective and the transformation of a biblical commandment takes place (Mark 7:9–13). A fundamental community value has been changed into a groundless custom, full of hypocrisy and with profound social implications. Although the law of Moses is very explicit, indicating for such situations even very harsh measures in relation to the honouring of parents, the tradition of the people changed things to an almost ridiculous situation. The recognition of parents involved only a formal gesture, the mechanical repetition of a protocol cliché, and no longer entailed concrete acts to demonstrate respect and esteem for them. For Jesus, this represents a concrete case of the invalidation of God's law, in effect its abolition. The lesson emphasized here by the teacher is essential for the formation of disciples. The issue itself is not the replacement of divine truth by a norm of human weakness and convenience, but rather the implications that flow from this. When the fundamentals are abandoned, things break down at their core, at the level of the source that animates and gives content to human experience. Neglect of parents is not only a matter of convenience or even contempt from the younger generation, but also something that undermines the future, a rupture in the community that makes the process of passing on values difficult or almost impossible.

Another example of this kind of drift is found in Mark 10, where the subject of marriage and the possibility of divorce is raised (Mark 10:1–12). In this case, forgetting the fundamentals involves a long series of deeply destructive slippages. The blindness that is specific to this process of dilution leads people not to notice the effects, but to justify their situation, to construct new rules and formal mechanisms to ensure their legitimacy. In Jesus's reply to the leaders, we see the exercise of common sense that must be used in any problem, namely, to refer to the source, to the foundations (in this case not just quoting from the biblical text, but emphasising the truth it contains), and then to evaluate the tradition and possible solutions in the light of these.

The second stage of Jesus's response takes place without specifying the presence of religious leaders (Mark 7:14–23). It seems that they have not fully understood what Jesus has said in the previous speech and are intrigued by a sapiential expression that sums up his teaching on the theme of human purity: "there is nothing outside a person that by going into him can defile him, but the things that come out of a person are what defile him" (Mark 7:15). Jesus's explanatory commentary on this phrase may seem curious, and to argue for a form of dualism, for he points out that what a person eats or drinks is not important for his purity, but only what is in the heart, that is, evil thoughts and intentions, passions and shameful deeds. But an emphasis in the text indicates that the teacher actually wanted to remove the barrier imposed by the law of Moses regarding clean and unclean food, without having committed a shift of emphasis from the sensible to the unseen world. For Jesus, the idea that it is not certain foods that make a person unclean, but evil thoughts and deeds, seems like common sense, a reality accessible to anyone. But even for the scholars of the time, and even for ordinary people like Jesus's disciples, things were not so clear. The master reproaches the disciples for their lack of understanding in this matter. We are witnessing a form of blindness that is linked to the undiscerning and narrow-minded practice of a tradition that comes from the past. The indulgence in forms and false spirituality under their shelter is a constant temptation for any community of believers. The process of formation must take such elements into account, so that discipleship frequently involves a twofold effort: first, identifying and demolishing badly built structures, residues left over from the distortion of the mechanism of tradition, rules and prescriptions born out of various human interests; second, rebuilding forgotten or lost values and principles, and assimilating new truths that can be understood in the present context of God's economy.

Another important episode to which the disciples are exposed concerns the theme of the foreigner and the relation of Jews to another ethnic group. We are dealing with a sensitive subject and a rich experiential heritage in the history of the Jewish people. Jesus is confronted with this interesting situation when a Syro-Phoenician woman asks him to heal her child, a girl possessed by a demon (Mark 7:24–30). Jesus's response to the woman's request may be scandalous to some. We have become accustomed to a benevolent and merciful teacher, full of compassion for those in trouble. Suddenly he becomes serious and seemingly racist, insulting the woman. What is really going on? By the brave and wise response that this woman articulates – a foreigner to the promises of the house of Israel – we realize that the teacher's comment is intentional. The disciples are thus witnessing a test that the teacher applies to an outsider who has had the courage to approach him. For the disciples, the opportunity is extraordinary, and the whole picture is incredible. Although Jesus uses the theme of the foreigner by appealing to a Jewish cliché that treats those of a different ethnicity as a second-class priority, everything changes with the woman's response. Where does the foreign woman's strength of character and wisdom come from? Could it just be her distress and desire to find a solution for her child? Or did her status as a foreigner harden her personality and make her able to see in Jesus more than a Jew contemptuous of those of another race? Mark tells us that Jesus appreciated the woman's words, and implicitly her attitude and faith, so he fulfils her request and sends her home to her daughter. The biblical text tells us nothing about the disciples, but we can guess that they witnessed the whole scene with puzzlement. The training process also involves this way of learning by witnessing the trials of others. We are looking at a character who had every reason to be neglected, treated with contempt, and rejected (we know that Jews had phobias about both public interactions with women and public contact with people of other ethnicities). Overcoming one's own condition and assuming that faith is a profoundly human capacity that transcends all social barriers must have marked the disciples. They themselves began to be labelled and looked upon with suspicion because they were disciples of Jesus, a strange man who disregarded traditions and official authorities. The woman in this story is an example for the disciples and for us today. The condition of the foreigner and traveller becomes paradigmatic for the community of Jesus's disciples. For those who decided to follow him, identity no longer depends on social, economic, political, religious, ethnic, gender, and other constraints, but only on discipleship, defined by the faith, values, and mission of the master.

Finally, we refer to an important episode in the training of disciples. It takes place in the context of a discussion in which Jesus asks the apostles what people think of him, and then asks them what they think of his identity. The dialogue is succinctly recounted in Mark 8, in the characteristic style of the Gospel of Mark. As an approach, we seem to be dealing with a double exercise – checking and fixing what they have understood. The setting is private, but in motion. On a mission on a road between the villages of Galilee, the teacher asks this strange question (Mark 8:27–29). Is he really interested in what people say about him? Does he sense some crisis or problem in the public perception of himself and his mission? Or is this essential for the disciples and their training? From the answer Jesus received, it seems that the subject is a really important one for the dynamics of discipleship. The identification of Jesus with John the Baptist or the prophet Elijah is in line with the messianic expectations of the Jewish people, but it is a false lead. The disciples probably heard people saying such things about their teacher, which caused confusion. It is clear that Jesus did not care about his image, did not want people to have a certain opinion of him, but he certainly had expectations of his disciples. It is not easy to follow a master about whom a lot of things are said and to whom various false images are associated. Certain ideas about Jesus seemed justified, because he acted according to a pattern specific to prophets and with an authority that people had begun to recognize. But what they understood was not correct. This is of utmost importance to the teacher. You cannot be a genuine disciple if you do not know deeply the person of the master, and know what his identity and mission really are. For Jesus, transparency to his disciples was always a priority. Even if they frequently did not understand him and always needed to restructure their thoughts and expectations of him, by the way the teacher related to them and discipled them, he aimed to create a deep and profound bond between them. Peter, one of the Twelve, gave an answer that satisfied Jesus. The fact that they recognized him as the Messiah or the Christ, the messenger of God, is a sign that they are on the right path, even if it is not quite clear what they meant by this. Although there were many images and even preconceptions about this messenger of God, for Jesus it is enough that the disciples are close to him and open to accept this identity of his. Even if it does not fit the patterns of the people or the expectations of the leaders, for his disciples Jesus is considered the Christ. It is a solid biblical identity that provides the foundation for the discipleship relationship and for the complex and ongoing work of formation, stability for the difficult moments, joy for the moments of rest, and encouragement for the mission to come.

Regardless of the stage of the apprenticeship, the training work aims at developing the apprentice's being and at shaping as clearly as possible a solid relationship with the teacher. Sometimes the emphasis is on the foundations and the assumption of a consistent body of knowledge resulting from a coherent understanding of Scripture and the experience of the elders. At other times, the focus is on the practical side, on getting involved in action and acquiring skills for a particular mission. If we follow Jesus's pedagogical strategy with his disciples, we see that the two are always intertwined and that neither is neglected. As they advance on their journey with Christ, the disciples take up in various forms the fundamentals of the faith, and participate with the teacher in his mission. Along the way, the understanding of Jesus's identity matures and is challenged in many ways. Essential, however, is the nature and stability of the relationship between the two parties. It can only be based on trust and the clarity of the transformations that take place in the life of the follower of Jesus. In every historical place and epoch, Christian discipleship involves this process of actualizing the principles of biblical revelation in new contexts of human experience and accepting their transformative authority. But this cannot be done without appeal to the experience of our precursors, to their efforts to understand, and to what they achieved as disciples of the Lord, including their mistakes.

Questions

1. In the examples of discipleship that you know, what is more emphasized: the acquisition of knowledge, the acquisition and use of ministry skills, or the development of the whole personality?

2. How important is the idea of personal development in the community you are part of?

3. How is Christian identity defined in your own ecclesial context?

4. What is the role of church tradition in your own Christian life?

5. What about in the life of the ecclesial community you belong to?

6. Does Jesus's model of personality function as an ideal in your life? How do you understand his role as a real model for Christian life?

11

The Tests of Discipleship

After the disciples return from their mission (Mark 6), the evangelist records a succession of miracles and confrontations between Jesus and the Jewish scholars. The disciples also participate in all this in various ways: either actively, in the multiplication of the loaves (Mark 6:30–44; 8:1–9), or passively, in the crossing of the Sea of Galilee (Mark 6:45–52) and Jesus's disputes with the Pharisees (Mark 7:1–13; 8:10–12). Despite the progress made in the discipleship process, the evangelist points out several times (in Mark 6 and 8) that the teacher reproaches the disciples for not really understanding what they see and hear. From the text of Scripture, it is obvious that Jesus has certain expectations of the disciples in terms of their participation in his mission and especially in terms of shaping their understanding. Scripture does not make clear what this knowledge was to be, nor how it was to be used by the apostles in the concrete situations in which they took part. Rather, in response to Jesus's reproach, Mark feels obliged to add an explanation for the lack of receptivity of the Twelve: they were hard-hearted (Mark 8:17). This is an Old Testament formula that requires careful interpretation. Here, however, we have an invitation to investigate how to gain understanding through discipleship, and what might impede the disciple from reaching this goal. In the way he thinks and acts, Jesus seems to appeal to the strategy of testing, of evaluating disciples with specific tools and clear objectives.

Before looking at some of the tests to which Jesus subjects his disciples, we might examine their role in the discipleship process, and possibly when the assessments are used by the master. As in other areas of human experience, tests come at the end of certain stages, at moments of transition to another stage. Their role is to establish what stage of the process the person being assessed is at, to highlight both what has been achieved and what is missing. If we look carefully at Jesus's way of working, we can see that the teacher is very demanding with the disciples and very strict in his evaluation. He seems harsh, expecting too much and demanding results too quickly. But for discipleship, realism and seriousness of evaluation are very important. Direct and transparent confrontation with what the apprentices have become, what they know and what skills they have acquired is an essential tool in the process. No matter what the disciple's reaction and perception of this assessment may be, this aspect of the relationship with the master cannot be negotiated. The purpose of testing is not to point out weaknesses and what has not been done, but to reveal how much real learning has taken place and how profound the disciple's transformation is.

Mark comments on what Jesus understood – that the disciples did not understand the miracle of the multiplication of the loaves (Mark 6:52). This remark is made in the context of a more special miracle taking place in private, away from the gaze of the crowds. The whole scene seems to be carefully staged to prepare for a test that was very well planned by the teacher. Thus, after the multiplication of the loaves, Jesus sends the crowds home, advises the disciples to cross the Sea of Galilee, and he climbs the mountain alone to pray (Mark 6:45–51). The image alludes to an Old Testament biblical episode in which Moses goes up the mountain to meet God, and the leaders are left alone to deal with the people's problems. In both scenes, things are rushed, take an undesirable turn, and come to an unfortunate end. In the case of the disciples, they are at sea and rowing hard, they seem overwhelmed by the situation, and need help. Then they see Jesus coming on the water. It looks like the solution has come just in time and they will be easily rescued. Yet, Jesus wants to pass by them (or pretends to pass by the boat), but the disciples see him, get scared and think they are dealing with a ghost (*phantasma*). After Jesus gets into the boat and stops the wind, he speaks to the disciples and tells them to have faith, not to be afraid. The whole episode unfolds quickly, photographically, and the effect is that the disciples remain frozen, without reply, incapable of any concrete action. The scene is very visual, dense, like something out of a surrealist film. No one expected Jesus to appear in this way, hence the surprising response of the apostles. The moral of the text seems to suggest that the disciples' reaction was not as it should have been, that they failed the test and that the master expected something else. What, then, would have been the desired behaviour, the mature reaction? What did the disciples miss in the lesson on the multiplication of the loaves which left them unable to handle the event on the sea and the appearance of Jesus differently? What did it mean that their hearts were hardened?

Failure in the exam shows that perhaps something has not yet been dislodged in the apprentice's being. The experiences the master went through were enlightening, and one would expect that they would generate a deeper kind of transformation, a certain maturity. It is precisely such a leap that is targeted by the master's tests. But the work does not come by itself, it requires analysis, evaluation, and highlighting of what is not working well. So, later on, when the disciples return full of enthusiasm from a mission, instead of being commended for their deeds and encouraged, they are subjected to an examination that they do not pass, and are then faced with a disarming conclusion. Is the master too demanding, we may ask?

The scene of the multiplication of the loaves shows us how things really are in the process of discipleship. The disciples have participated in so many extraordinary experiences with their teacher, they themselves have worked miracles on the missionary journey. Faced with the need to feed the crowds, the only solution they came up with was to send the hungry to the villages to buy food. The fact that they dared do nothing else – they could even ask for a miracle – shows that what the teacher had hoped for had not yet been realized in their being. The hardened heart corresponds to a rigid, flattened being in which becoming is not actualized. This hardening does not have to do with the lack of knowledge of a rational proposition, of a theological truth (such as the divinity of Jesus), but rather with a lack of trust, of a deep knowledge of the teacher, a lack of courage to go closer to him and to go out of oneself for this step. The disciples witness miracles as common religious and cultural experiences specific to their age and religious tradition. Even though they declared him to be the Messiah, it is possible that, for them, Jesus was still just a rabbi, at best an extravagant one who does many interesting things, but his true identity did not pierce them, did not lead to a significant change in their own identity. Their wonderment and their shuddering at the miracles are the usual signs of a person not sufficiently penetrated by the true faith, or who is instilled with a shallow faith that is always in need of signs and wonders. The tests of Jesus seem to point to some deficiencies in the structure of the disciples: they seemed unable to go beyond custom and cultural context; they were living the life of discipleship with a sort of detachment which comes from the almost mechanical assumption of a knowledge based on tradition, both about the process of discipleship and about the master; they displayed no creative force at work, nothing original in thought or expression, no concrete personal stake; no glimmer that goes beyond the beaten horizon of ordinary religious expectations.

It should also be noted that the disciples failed a test when the teacher was not near them and in a rather complicated context: night, tiredness, a rough sea, intense wind, disorientation. Did they feel abandoned? Did this experience – lived in the absence of the master – come too soon? Or can we understand this test as part of the teacher's strategy of slowly preparing the disciples for the difficult stage of separation? Very possibly so. The master's concern is to support the development of well-rounded personalities, not ones that always need the tutelage specific to the period of spiritual childhood. He wants his disciples to reach maturity, not to be stuck in the process and incapable of exercising their own freedom. Sending the followers out to sea alone is a gesture that anticipates sending them out into the world, without the assistance of their teacher. The biblical text is suggestive and emphasizes that Jesus sent them ahead of him across the sea, just as he had previously sent the apostles through the towns of Galilee, where they used the authority given by Jesus and worked miracles. Presumably the teacher expected that even in this sending they would assume what they had received, put into practice what they had seen in their teacher, and complete their journey well. The lesson of this test seems to be related to the ability of the disciples to carry out the entrusted mission without the physical presence of the teacher, and to use with confidence what they had received from him. Though this did not happen, it does not mean that nothing changed in their beings, that they did not really benefit from the authority given to them in their mission. Rather, we note that the process of formation is not over, and that time and concrete lessons are still needed for that growth in maturity.

Jesus's second warning to the disciples that they do not understand and are hard-hearted occurs after the new miracle in which Jesus multiplies the loaves and fishes for a second time, and after a dispute the teacher had with the Pharisees (Mark 8:1–21). Using the metaphor of leaven (which, in the context, has a negative biblical meaning), Jesus draws the disciples' attention to the ability of the Pharisees and King Herod to corrupt and influence people with harmful ideas and dangerous teachings. The disciples' response to this profound message of Jesus is described by Mark as typical of unbelievers discussing among themselves their own understanding and rejecting what was offered by the teacher. The master's commentary on what the disciples say is one borrowed from the Old Testament, a message addressed by God to those who do not listen to the prophetic word and do not fulfil it. The Pharisees and Herod were the most prominent exponents of the category of those who do not believe in Jesus and reject his message because of their hardened hearts. Jesus's question – "Are your hearts hardened?" – is rhetorical and challenges the disciples to assess their situation. The teacher is uncomfortable; the warning is tailor-made because he warns of the danger of ignorance to those who do not believe in him and oppose him. This assessment takes place in the context of the tradition of the Jewish people, and shows the difficulty the disciples must overcome in order to acquire a different understanding of God and his work with humanity.

In the way events are presented by the evangelist, we can notice a very interesting approach of the teacher to the training of the disciples. Repetition is not the mother of teaching, as the saying goes, but it is an opportunity to reread certain aspects of unlearned lessons. The biblical text tells us that the second scene of the multiplication of the loaves is repeated almost identically to the first: the identification of a need, a challenge by the master, and a totally inadequate response by the disciples. It is as if this story never happened the first time. The same opacity and lack of prompt response again characterize the disciples. No one seems to have remembered the previous scene, no one mentions the first miracle, no one had the courage to mention that Jesus's presence with them was already a solution. This lack of understanding, this ignorance of the disciples, is absolutely dazzling. How can you forget a miracle in which you fed five thousand men with five loaves of bread and two fish and collected twelve baskets of scraps? Almost annoyed, the teacher formulates a series of rhetorical questions about the inability of the disciples to see, hear, and remember. It is an appeal to the disciple's senses, not those for the sensible world, but those that open the being to meaning, discernment, and a reception of the things behind events. Jesus's criticism is difficult to describe, because it is painful. After all this, the master asks, "Do you still not understand?"

The warning about discipleship seems clear enough now. On the one hand, the realism of the process is highlighted. It involves an effort on both sides, teacher and disciple, with risks and challenges. No one offers any guarantees for a particular end because it requires commitment and freedom on the relational level and openness for transformation on the level of being. Building one up as a disciple is not an easy process. It takes effort, tests, and failures, comebacks and evaluations, the toil of explanation and confrontation, a kind of energy and craftsmanship on the part of the teacher so that things do not become hopeless. A real danger is imitation, the mechanics of banal experience, and the formulation of false expectations. On the other hand, we are warned about the stakes of the process. Discipleship is not just a mechanism for receiving a body of knowledge or an effort to acquire some practical skills. We are in fact talking about a process of transformation of the apprentice's being, a becoming of the disciple that leads to a different perspective on reality and the meaning of existence. It is a profound change that brings new meanings to the dynamics of existence as a whole and to the events of everyday life. The understanding that is built up in discipleship has to do with a substantial transformation of the apprentice's mode of existence and a recalibration of all the faculties by which he perceives the complexity of reality and relates to it.

For today's disciple, the idea of faith-testing is familiar from Scripture and church tradition, but it is rarely encountered in the dynamics of discipleship. Who is responsible for constructing and applying these tests today? Do we leave it all to divine economy and consider that it is for God to test our faith, or do we accept other ways of applying tests? Are contemporary disciples educated in this spirit of evaluation and taking tests to strengthen their identity and mission?

As a rule, through a careful exercise of analysing the road we have travelled, we can identify a series of such tests that God has put us through, and intuit what lessons needed to be learned. This looking back is easier to design if it is done with someone more mature, to whom the disciples are willing to open their lives, and participate in evaluation work. The model of Jesus's relationship with the apostles encourages us to take up the pedagogy of testing in discipleship relationships among believers as well. This important aspect for the transformation of the human person we find sometimes in relationships between those who love each other, or in other kinds of relationships in which people invest seriously.

Tests are important not only for giving impetus and rhythm to the process of becoming a disciple, but also because they are like stones or remembrance, essential landmarks on the path of faith, places where one could return in moments of difficulty. Even if these are uncomfortable and very demanding, the acceptance of the economy of the tests in the process of discipleship is an act of normality and must be a basic tool in the life of any disciple of Jesus.

Questions

1. What are the main stages you have gone through in your discipleship or life of faith?

2. Did you ever receive help to evaluate yourself or did you have to analyse these stages later on your own?

3. Have you ever faced discouragement in your life of faith? How did you overcome it?

4. How do you practically relate to the challenges Jesus or a mentor have given to your Christian life?

5. How do you manage the presence of Jesus as a master in your daily life?

6. What does it mean to you that in the life of discipleship the stake is the becoming of your whole self?

7. How important are freedom and creativity in the discipleship process for the master under whose authority you have been formed?

12

Preparing for Separation from the Teacher

An important change takes place in Jesus's work, and in his relationship with his disciples, from the moment the Saviour begins to speak to the Twelve about his passion and death. Before his triumphal entry into Jerusalem, the Gospel of Mark mentions three times (Mark 8:31; 9:31; 10:33) that the teacher opened his heart to the disciples and told them about what awaited him at the end of his mission: he would be rejected by the leaders of the Jewish people; he would be condemned to death for things he had not done; he would be beaten and mocked by the people; he would be killed, but on the third day he would rise from the dead. We saw that the master had already begun the work of preparing the disciples for the final stage of separation and for the period that would follow his departure. Events were starting along the straight line towards the last part of Jesus's mission and the final lessons for the disciples. From the biblical text, we can see that the intensity of the discipleship process now reaches new heights. The topics discussed are deeper, the disciples' questions show a different level of maturity, and the teacher's challenges are even more serious. As we shall see, at this stage Jesus resumes the fundamentals of discipleship, reaffirms the paradigm of his own mission, and invites the disciples to an evaluation of what they have understood and their readiness to implement the values required by the master.

After Jesus's first confession of the events to come in Jerusalem (Mark 8:31), there is a public discourse on a subject that the disciples and the audience probably did not expect. Jesus seems increasingly firm and determined to settle things about the stakes of his mission. He states emphatically that the meaning of all existence depends on how a person responds to the invitation to follow him, to be his disciple. Here we see an opening of the horizon of discipleship for all those who are willing to accept the call and the demands of the Saviour:

85

"If anyone would come after me, let him deny himself and take up his cross and follow me" (Mark 8:34). The text continues with a message with soteriological and eschatological connotations, but the key remains the reference to Jesus Christ, the acceptance of his identity and the assumption of his discipleship. Two important things are emphasized in the teacher's invitation presented in the text of this Gospel.

The first is suggested by the paradoxical statement in the first part of the biblical quotation. It takes will and freedom to become a disciple of Jesus, but at the same time it requires a decision to renounce oneself completely. Absolute respect for the freedom of the human person is the basis of Christian discipleship and the spirituality that is built on this way of life. When this freedom is violated or confiscated by institutional or power mechanisms, the legitimacy of the use of the status of Christian or disciple of God is also lost. This foundation of discipleship is an essential reference point for the community that is born out of the life and mission of the teacher. Equally, to become a disciple of Jesus is a profound act of self-denial, of renouncing one's own way of life. Discipleship implies the assumption of a new identity, a becoming that demands from the human being a total abandonment, a total openness to transformation and the construction of a new status. Being a disciple means to have a special relationship with the teacher and to belong to a community that bases its way of life on a particular value system. All this builds a new life and a new meaning of existence, a new way of understanding reality and participating in it.

The second aspect concerns the assumption of the human condition and the mission of the teacher. The biblical text uses the phrase "take up his cross" to create this correspondence between the experience of any disciple and that of the teacher. The vocation of the disciple is to live a life according to the same principles, standards, and values that Jesus showed us in his life. The status of disciple is always confirmed by the actualization of the master's work and by the expression of a life that always keeps the teacher as source and model. The phrase used by Jesus includes the suggestive term "cross." It prophetically encompasses two aspects. On the one hand, it refers to the experience of suffering and death that Jesus will undergo, deriving from Jesus's decision to renounce himself and place himself totally under God's authority. On the other hand, it implies the master's expectation that the disciple would be willing to assume a similar condition in the world. Bearing the cross means assuming one's own sacrifice, the radical transformation of the self and the acceptance of the responsibility and mission that comes from embodying the teacher's values. Following Christ may involve profound self-change and all that comes with that status, including suffering and persecution, opposition and malice from people, harsh conditions of service, or even the ultimate price of giving one's life for one's neighbour.

Another aspect emphasized by the biblical text regarding Jesus's testimony of what is to come in Jerusalem is that the disciples do not understand this message in depth (Mark 9:32). They can neither understand how such a tragic end of the master is possible, nor the implications of this scenario for what is to come. On the contrary, the disciples have begun to have discussions about who will be greater among them after the teacher's departure. Therefore, they stick to what they know best – the model of a rabbinical school of that time. If the master leaves, it means that a new management is needed to take the school forward, and the role of the apprentices is to ensure that this project continues through a decision related to the delegation of authority. In response to their concern, Jesus teaches them a lesson with at least two important points that need to be clarified. First, the teacher redefines the idea of primacy, that of being the greatest or the head, the leader or authority over others. We are witnessing a paradigm shift that puts the emphasis on service, on the willingness to serve all. It is clear that this message concerns Christ himself first and then all who choose to be his disciples. The community built around the master is grounded on the foundation of discipleship; but its absolute novelty is the essential value of serving others, of unconditional love of neighbour. Only those who understand and embrace such a definition of discipleship can follow Jesus. Second, the teacher demonstrates to the end the authenticity and solidity of his mission. He acknowledges God's sending and authority in his life, as manifested explicitly in the forms recognized by Jewish tradition (through the biblical text, through the people and prophets, and through what he said and did). Discipleship in the school of Jesus presupposes the existence of a framework that confirms and validates the authority of the teacher and gives each disciple the opportunity to anchor him or herself in the context of a solid and enduring tradition. The following of Christ involves enrolment in a chain of discipleship, with experiences that link from one generation to the next and give continuity to the mission and spirit of the teacher. The principles and values of the master remain relevant in the world through a succession of disciples and teachers who have decided to live their lives after the model of Jesus and are ready to put into others what they have received.

The third mention of Jesus's passion (Mark 10:33–34) takes place in the context of the approach to Jerusalem, after some intense discussions between the disciples and the teacher. The Twelve are increasingly affected by what they hear, by the master's expectations of marriage and wealth (see the confrontation with the Pharisees and the rich young man), and they consider that what is being asked of them is beyond human capabilities (Mark 10:17–27). What's more, the proximity of Jerusalem troubles them beyond measure, so that the journey becomes almost an agony. The biblical text tells us that the disciples followed Jesus in a state of fear, listening to the same message about the death of the teacher in the holy city, witnessing speeches that are very hard to digest, and that turn the human mind and heart upside down. In this tense state, one thing seems important and concerns two of Christ's closest disciples. They have questions about the future and the end of life, the eschatological times. The two courageous brothers, James and John, want assurances about the end of the road and the results of their election. They want to be like the teacher, to share with him the honours at the end of the mission (Mark 10:35–40). In other words, the biblical text brings us into this sensitive situation of evaluating discipleship, of being able to anticipate the end of the road. It seems that the disciples have assimilated well the ancient wisdom that the disciple is called to become like the teacher and share in his glory. And it was also quite clear from the ancient wisdom of antiquity that the disciples can share in such glory if they strictly follow the way of the teacher. Only, in the case of Jesus, things seem to go much deeper. He proposes a different model of teacher and a different way of fulfilling the mission. That is why he asks his disciples if they are willing to pay the same price that the teacher is ready to pay in Jerusalem; if they are open to following the path of discipleship according to standards that are completely different from the spirit of the age. The biblical text tells us nothing about Jesus's reaction to what he heard from the two disciples, who agreed that they could follow in the master's footsteps to the end. We would expect him to praise them, to be proud of their positive response and the openness with which they declare their readiness to follow the teacher in all things. But if we follow the line of the text, the master shifts the discussion to himself. Even though he is the teacher and the authority over the disciples, Christ assumes to the end the role of servant sent by the Father. Jesus responds that God is the absolute authority and that he has the prerogative of rewarding the disciples. At this moment of evaluation and reaching the moment of parting, it is the teacher who humbles himself and, in this way, lifts up the disciples. He thus becomes the bridge between humanity and God, the guarantor that the standards demanded of the disciples, which have been judged impossible for humans to achieve, are still possible to be achieved thanks to what Christ is accomplishing in the world. In this way the master sets himself as the keystone and foundation for the new human experience as disciple of Christ.

At the end of the discussion opened by John and James, the text returns to the new paradigm of the relationship between disciples and to the model of the true master, the exemplarity of total service (Mark 10:42–45). The teacher speaks to the future and looks to the community formed on the discipleship experience of the Twelve. He hopes that his project will endure, that what he has achieved will be carried forward. He is willing to pay the ultimate price, to lay down his life for his disciples, for all those who freely and understandingly want to follow his path. On this sacrifice is built the value of discipleship and the good news of Scripture.

In the face of his own suffering, near the end of the road, the teacher brings an extra note of depth to discipleship. He emphasizes that it is built on the supreme sacrifice of the master, on the gift of his life to the people who wish to follow him, for the whole world he calls to himself. Now the picture of discipleship is almost complete. Following Christ rests on the solid foundation of total love that conquers all, including death, and is sealed with the blood of the teacher. The hope for the future that disciples will make other disciples in history is based on the strength of Christ's example, on the power of the new life lived in the presence of God, on what has been built up relationally between the teacher and the Twelve, on the trust placed in the people from one generation to the next that light conquers darkness and freedom conquers sin. It is with this courage that other disciples in all places and times grow and embrace the mission of Jesus. The living community of the teacher lives on the foundation of discipleship that always feeds from the life of Jesus.

Questions

1. To what extent can discipleship remain an existential goal for a disciple, even after separation from the mentor?

2. What do we learn from Jesus's disciples in relation to the theme of their separation from him?

3. How prepared do you feel to part ways with your mentor? Or how prepared do you think that you were if it has already happened?

4. What makes you feel prepared or unprepared to mentor others?

5. How do you assess the need for authority in your life even after you have left your mentor?

6. What might be the reasons for disciples delaying the parting of ways with their mentor?

7. What are possible negative aspects that could artificially accelerate or extend unnecessarily the discipleship relationship in the context of your own church community?

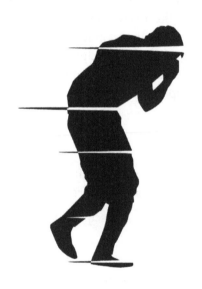

13

What We Learn when the Master is Tested

The last week of Jesus's life and work is important for discipleship in many ways. One interesting aspect to consider is how the disciples witness the evaluations and tests that the master himself endures as he nears the end of his mission. Any pupil or student would respond with the greatest satisfaction to the challenge of being present at an examination in which the teacher is the one being assessed. But the disciples of Jesus attend such assessments without being warned in detail, without actually knowing what is going to happen in Jerusalem, even though the teacher has told them of a tragic and totally incomprehensible end. In what follows, assuming the perspective of the disciples, we will examine a series of events that take place during the holy week in Jerusalem, with the teacher and his work at the centre. The tests to which Jesus is subjected are opportunities for the disciples to learn new lessons, more profound and not easy to assimilate.

A first test for the teacher is about his true identity and people's expectations of the Messiah. In the Gospel of Mark, the scene of the entry into Jerusalem is briefly presented, and the focus falls on a number of details that engage the disciples particularly in the organization of the event (Mark 11:1–10). The teacher does not explain anything about what is to follow but sends two of the disciples to bring a donkey and gives them much precise information about the identification of the animal and the eventual reaction of the owners. It seems quite clear that the biblical author's intention is to show important behind-the-scenes elements of the event and to underline the prophetic dimension of the action. The festive event of Jesus's arrival in the capital is presented much more briefly (in just three verses). The teacher seems to get involved in the logic of the crowd waiting for him in the holy city as the Messiah, but he does so in his own style. Perhaps for the disciples this was confusing: Jesus is being prepared for a triumphal entry into Jerusalem, worthy of a great king, but he seems only halfway into the game. The Messiah's ascent to the stage is in the spirit of the prophet Zechariah, that is, in humility, peace, and righteousness. Jesus literally fulfils the prophecy of the past and enters the city on a donkey. The biblical text tells us nothing either about Jesus's reaction to the cheers of the crowd or about how the disciples experienced the scene. On this occasion, the teacher himself is subjected to a test, to a great challenge. He accepts the title of Messiah, but not in the image and expectation of the Jewish people or their leaders, but in the spirit of Scripture. Jesus rejects the image of a glorious leader and assumes the condition of a humble servant who has come to do God's will, not that of the people. The way in which the master assumes his identity as Messiah is also a key lesson for the disciples. They are called to follow Jesus in the same paradigm of service, in humility and total dedication to God. Whoever wishes to be a disciple of Christ must be willing and able to overcome the temptation of the glory of this world, the desire for power and domination, the acclaim of the crowd, and the benefits of a superior position as leader of the people in the name of the Lord.

Another time when the master is subject to public evaluation is when the religious authorities demand an account of his work (Mark 11:15–18). The teacher takes his role as a prophet of God seriously and exercises his authority in the house of God. Although he has visited the temple before and seen all the religious commerce that goes on there, he now has the context to take a stand and deliver his own message. Obviously, to challenge what is going on in the temple is to challenge the authority of the priests and religious leaders, the whole system of religion of the chosen people. Such an attitude could not be without consequences. Jesus already had a reputation as an atypical prophet, a man who did not respect the ancient customs and who had gathered numerous complaints from the synagogues of the cities through which he passed. But in Jerusalem things take on a special significance. As a result, the priests and scribes decide to confront Jesus in the temple and put him to a new test. He is asked by what authority (*exousia*) he does what he does, and who gave him this authority. The question seems simple, and Jesus's answer could be given immediately. But the teacher avoids a direct answer and, in accordance with Jewish custom, responds with his own challenge and asks a question of his own. For the disciples, such a tactic is probably not new. In those days, theological disputes between rabbis were common, and such strategies were employed routinely. But what Jesus does is not only an appeal to a debating technique, but also a way of answering a test that is not as simple as it seems.

Why wasn't it enough for Jesus to respond directly and say that he has authority from God? First, because his answer also required a justification. Neither Jesus nor any other teacher can base his authority on himself or on what he does alone. That is why he asked religious leaders to examine the person and work of John the Baptist, the one who testified to Jesus's identity. Second, because those confronting Jesus were the official authorities, those who had the power to recognize the teacher's ministry, but these leaders were in their own state of blindness and would not allow their position to be challenged. Jesus thus put them in the difficult position of giving an answer which, if honest, also implicitly constituted the truth about his authority. From the perspective of the disciples, we have a new lesson that can be highlighted by the masterful way in which the teacher responds. Jesus does not defend his position and mission, does not struggle to demonstrate his status as rabbi or teacher, prophet, or servant of the Lord. The identity and authority of Jesus come along the lines of the prophets, as confirmed by John the Baptist and the Scriptures, by God himself through his manifestation. The refusal of the priests and scribes to give a response, which was obvious, shows once again (as with John) the lack of authenticity of their authority and their inability to challenge Jesus's authority. For the teacher, there is a testimony attesting to his authority, but for those in charge of the temple, there is only an authority resulting from the status of the office, a formal one, which is not intrinsic and is without support in what they are and what they do.

Another very interesting test for the teacher is related to his natural limits and physiological needs (Mark 11:12–14, 20–26). The Gospel tells us that the day after the triumphal entry into the holy city, Jesus and the disciples were again on their way to Jerusalem, and the teacher was hungry. Jesus saw a fig tree from a distance and went near it to look for fruit to eat but found nothing. The biblical text mentions that it was not yet fig season and that it was normal not to find any. What follows, however, is no longer reasonable for the human mind. Jesus's attitude and reaction seem to show that the teacher failed a trivial test. How do you curse an innocent tree? Simply put, it was not the season for the fig tree. Why does Jesus have unfounded expectations? Isn't his attitude an action in anger, a reaction of a man in need betraying his dissatisfaction? The Gospel of Mark briefly reports that the disciples heard and recorded the words spoken by Jesus, but does not report any particular attitude. Even the next day, when the disciples saw that the fig tree had withered, they had no comment on the teacher's attitude. But suddenly everything turns into a lesson about faith.

The casual reader might ask, amazed, what the power of faith is here. If the teacher had had faith, he could have made the fig tree bear fruit, instead of cursing it so that it withered, and never bore fruit again. Can we fulfil our caprices by appealing to faith? It doesn't seem at all simple to take in this lesson about faith based on what Jesus accomplished. Regardless of whether or not he failed the test, the teacher focuses his attention on the disciples and tells them to have faith in God. What follows is a theologically dense biblical passage that contrasts sharply not only with the narrative approach of Mark 11, but also with Mark's style in general. Essentially, the biblical text presents faith as our ability to trust God when we ask something of him (a thing or his forgiveness). But this capacity is not an intrinsically human power, but one that develops relationally, according to a logic that derives from the coherent positioning of the human being in relation to God and to fellow human beings. Faith first commits us relationally to God and witnesses to his real presence with us in the world. It also commits us to our fellow human beings, and demands a different relationship to those with whom we live, such as forgiving those who have trespassed against us. Perhaps Jesus is using his own test of hunger and the fig tree to talk about faith and to point out that it requires a different kind of rationality and a different way of relating to reality. In human logic, what Jesus did to the fig tree makes no sense. But this is an opportunity for the teacher to point out that the believer's relationship to God and to his fellow people must be based on the logic of faith, not the wisdom of this world. Whoever does not make this leap and approaches the life of a disciple only by human reason and common sense, without putting faith to work, has no chance of fulfilling his destiny to become like his master.

The disciples have another opportunity to see the teacher at work when the Pharisees are sent to Jesus to tempt him with a question about paying the tax (Mark 12:13–17). Clearly the situation in which the teacher is placed is a delicate one: on the one hand, everyone was obliged to pay taxes to the political authorities; on the other hand, this authority is an illegitimate one, because Israel was under Roman occupation. Whatever answer Jesus gave would be inappropriate and could have brought him to trial. But the master proves wise, and uses a relatively simple strategy, but with an unequivocal result. Without going into elements of political theology, we point out that Jesus takes into account the fact that human existence involves reporting to political and divine authority, implicitly religious authority (the Jews paid 10 percent to the temple, a tax required by God in the law). The teacher does not discuss any particular relationship between the two but emphasizes that both are legitimate, and that each addresses a well-defined field of our existence. But when Jesus refers to the theme of the image on the coin, he points not only to the reality of Caesar's authority. He also suggests that man, who is created in the image of God, must consider the divine authority over his life. For the disciples, the main lesson is highlighted first by the distinction between the two types of authority, and then by the emphasis that people must have the capacity and discernment for a coherent relationship to both, even if they may sometimes come into conflict. The disciples live in a world organized according to the laws of Caesar, but at the same time they belong to the kingdom of heaven and live according to the laws of God. As disciples of Jesus, we are invited to learn from the master how to live this paradoxical condition without losing our identity and without slipping into crisis situations or extremes of all kinds.

We conclude this section with a discussion of two theological debates in which Jesus is engaged in the presence of his disciples (Mark 12:18–34). First the Sadducees and then a teacher of the law challenge Jesus with questions that test the teacher's ability to interpret Scripture. In the first case, at stake is the theme of the resurrection, which the Sadducees did not believe in and felt they had sufficient arguments to challenge. For the disciples, Jesus's response is a very important theological lesson that overturns the so-called logic of the Jewish scholars who believe that the future life continues on the same coordinates of life in history. The teacher appeals to Scripture and the power of God to argue the truth of the resurrection, and shows why the Sadducees are wrong. It is possible to see here an explicit presentation of the two sources of authority underlying the teaching for the Christian faith: the Bible and the living experience of the community of believers where the power of God is shown under the guidance and work of the Holy Spirit. In the second case, when the synagogue teacher asks the master what the greatest commandment is, Jesus's answer is surprising because he presents two commandments as the most important for people. The first concerns God, the relationship of the human being to the divine, and the second concerns humanity and relationships between fellow human beings. For the disciples, the theological lesson is clear: the conception of God determines the conception of the human being and society; it is not possible to speak of the relationship with God without considering the relationship with people. This answer seems to be a corrective to the Jews who focused almost exclusively on achieving the most sophisticated religious relationship with the divine but left out essential things about the human community and what should change in society as a result of faith in God.

The transparency of Scripture about how Jesus responds to various tests is very important for discipleship. The teacher also assumed the condition of a disciple, was himself rigorous and subject to a discipline of obedience, and followed a process of shaping an identity through obedience and dependence on God and recognition of the authority of the forefathers. The biblical text shows the seriousness with which the teacher tackles the problems that confront him, the confrontations in which he is involved, and the temptations and traps into which he is drawn by his adversaries. Nothing is theatrical, false, or preordained. We are looking at the life and hard work of a person who has struggled to remain true to the faith and mission he has embraced. All this is a living witness, a foundation and model for the faith life of disciples everywhere, and for the journey of discipleship during which tests and challenges are always arising.

Questions

1. How exactly does it change our perspective of Jesus if we accept that he himself was put to the test? How does it help us in our relationship with God that he was also subject to temptations and trials in this world?

2. How do we relate to a mentor who is transparent in his dealings with us versus one who keeps certain things to him or herself?

3. To what extent is the authority of mentor diminished if we learn that they too have had their own shortcomings? How much trust can we have in mentors who share their own weaknesses with us?

4. What are the things that intrigue you about the degree of transparency of spiritual leaders who have guided your Christian life?

5. In what ways do spiritual leaders or teachers in your community influence the openness and transparency of their disciples towards others?

14

The Condition of the Disciple in the World

The disciples' last week with the master is an intense period in which certain things are discussed about the experience that will follow after their separation from him. In several prophetic texts, the Gospel of Mark summarizes a series of messages about the disciples' condition in the world, especially in relation to major apocalyptic events. The biblical text refers to the difficult period Israel will go through; then the perspective broadens and the discussion turns to the eschatological times of Jesus's return (Mark 13). To a large extent, these are exhortations to vigilance and discernment, training and watchfulness so that all things to come will find the disciples ready and able to face any challenge. Interestingly, the evangelist does not mention concrete things that the disciples have to do after the teacher leaves. It is implied, in fact, that their identity as disciples of the teacher presupposes the continuation of his mission in the world and the bearing of a concrete witness to the person of Jesus and what he has done for people. At his departure, Jesus seems more interested in giving the disciples an overview of what is to come, with the tensions and dangers that they will face. We do not sense in the teacher any hint of doubt about the disciples' faith and ability to face these adversities and to honour their commitment and status. Rather he compresses history and announces his return, the meeting at the end of time, the hope of reunion with his disciples and that, despite the difficulties, they will be ready for that meeting. It is a perspective that highlights the hope of the teacher, the confidence in his disciples and the fact that their mission will not be swallowed up by history but will go on to the end.

To the disciples, the master's message probably seems rather strange. It is true that it contains a number of details specific to Jewish tradition and spirituality, perceptible to the disciples up to a point, but openness to the whole world and the prospect of such a difficult mission might require further explanation. The biblical text mentions several times the future hostility of the world to the disciples' mission and identity. Their association with Jesus and what he did in history seems to be the most important cause for their violent rejection, along with their actions and message. If at first the disciples are warned about the hostile reaction and attitude of the world's authorities (Mark 13:9), religious and political alike, later the master announces a generalized adverse attitude (Mark 13:13). To this opposition the disciples must respond with patience and with the assumption of a kind of suffering, of living in the world as people rejected and condemned by their fellow human beings It is interesting that the disciples ask nothing about this turn of events, about the logic of this condition in the world for those who follow the teacher. It is clear that it all depends on how the world will perceive Jesus, and his disciples will have to carry his stigma among their own kind. At the same time, we note that the disciples do not ask for clarification of this attitude of rejection from the people towards the teacher. But Jesus's message implicitly contains a number of explanations that the disciples seem to have grasped. At stake is the true identity of the teacher, his quality as Messiah or Christ, and the perspective he brought to the role of this providential person expected both by the Jews and by the whole world. A Messiah who accepts death as a sacrifice for all, a Christ who declares himself the servant of all and who calls for love, compassion, and service to others, is uncomfortable and something that the spirit of the world cannot accept.

Promoting such an understanding of God's true messenger engenders opposition, and to be his disciple and carry on his mission is to be received by people as the teacher was treated. Here is the mainstay of the disciple's life after separation from the master: the readiness and ability to keep alive the true identity of the teacher; the courage and strength to carry out his mission in spite of the hostility of the world and people's expectation of a different Messiah and a different image of discipleship; and vigilance in the face of great events in history, and the attempt of the authorities and the common people to hinder the disciples' mission, or to derail it and give it other coordinates. Faced with such a complex perspective, such difficult discipleship conditions, the teacher brings up elements that will support the disciple's life and mission in the world. The general message is one of vigilance, discernment, and the ability to understand what is happening. Jesus insists on some very clear points.

First, the teacher asks the disciples to be attentive to other people and their mission, to their claims to be messengers of the true Christ (Mark 13:6).

In other words, there is competition, there are other disciples promoting a teacher and a mission that claims the tradition of the Messiah. In particular, Jesus draws attention to the end age and messianic expectations, when people will be increasingly likely to seek and accept a saviour. Such candidates for the position of Christ will do great harm by their ability to deceive and respond to people's desire to see miracles and signs, quick solutions to their problems. The true disciples of the true Messiah will have to face these confusions and temptations because their task is not only to save themselves in the midst of trouble, but also to bear authentic witness to the Christian identity and mission entrusted to them by Jesus. Times of crisis and confrontation are not only tests for disciples, but also opportunities to expose false disciples and their ideas, to show the blindness of what they promise people. The master is realistic and does not hide these dangers from the disciples and the full force of human ideals and quests, even when they are directed towards ephemeral goals. The danger of deception is great not only because of the many appearances of so-called Messiahs, but above all because of human weakness and the pressure of events which demand quick solutions. Jesus emphasizes that many will be misled and that it is essential for disciples to be vigilant and keep their discernment. It is up to them to pass on the teaching about the true Christ, for they are the light the world needs. Therefore, the formation of disciples must continue with greater assiduity and lucidity, with effort and resources well used, avoiding temptations to become themselves possible saviours of the world.

Second, the teacher asks them to be vigilant with themselves, especially at times when they will be subjected to violent treatment from all the forces that govern this world, from the religious to the political and legal (Mark 13:9–11). The disciples are reminded of an essential truth about their status and vocation to carry forward the teacher's model of life. They are not advocating a cause that is the product of their own minds or interests, but that of the master. They are the bearers of a message they have received from God, and they must be convinced that the chances of success in this mission lie not only in their own effort and wisdom. To be a disciple of Jesus is to be aware of the uninterrupted accompaniment of the teacher, and that this assistance is the active presence of God who watches over the fulfilment of his economy in the world. The disciples are not deprived of their responsibility and freedom of action, but are reminded that their mission implies a partnership and that they are not on their own. The teacher's message that the Holy Spirit will inspire disciples in the hour of confrontation with the world's great leaders (Mark 13:11) does not encourage a lack of consistent discipleship training and commitment. Jesus's concern is that in these difficult, high-pressure moments, the disciples do not fall into despair or fear about what they will be able to say. It is very important to stress that at this point of tension Jesus adds to discipleship the dimension of the presence of the Holy Spirit with the disciples in the world. The role of this divine person in the mission of the disciples is that of *parakletos* (the one who goes forth and opens the way), the faithful partner of the disciples in the fulfilment of the work of Jesus Christ. Christian discipleship implies the assumption of this partnership and the willingness to follow always the path opened by the Holy Spirit. What Jesus accomplished in the world is constantly actualized in the disciples through the ministry of this divine, mysterious person. He works to ground the new life, to enable them to become continual followers of Christ, and to build a solid relationship with God. In the process, the disciples are themselves (not just what they do and say) a witness to the world. It is important for the teacher to emphasize that what matters is their status as children of God, as disciples who are becoming more and more like Jesus, their being renewed and transformed, which is ever closer to perfection thanks to their relationship with the teacher and other believers. This reality is not to be doubted, even if the adversary will always try to make them do so. The battle is not fought first and foremost on the terrain of the cleverness of arguments, but on that of the conviction with which the disciple constantly reaffirms his or her status.

Third, the master asks them to keep an open mind and always learn. History goes on its way under God's authority, and great events will take place and have something to say. For believers the ability to discern the transformations of history is an essential dimension of the disciple's condition in the world. In order to avoid the danger of deception and failure, disciples need to understand the spirit of society. Their openness to the signs of history must be actively manifested and maintained with effort and dedication. It would be easy for them to adopt a conformist stance that follows the trends and the voice of the majority, but it is very difficult to maintain an alert spirit, a keen mind, and a character faithful to the master and the ministry entrusted to them. Jesus draws particular attention to the end times, and advises disciples to be clear-headed and to take a firm stance in the face of major, complex events with global impact. With regard to the complex period that will precede his return, the teacher does not give specific details. He does not present scenarios to be followed, but only gives signs and warnings. To the probing question of the disciples who wanted to know when the end would be, the teacher again assumes his humble position as servant of the Father and leaves all things to God alone (Mark 13:32). In a gesture that confirms his humility and his quality as a genuine servant, the master insists on the matters that are our responsibility. The emphasis falls on being exemplary disciples, on witnessing to serve faithfully at all times, no matter how much the world is shaking and how severe are the events around us. Discipleship frees us from the pressure of the end, from the obsession of knowing when and how things will happen. The disciple's orientation towards this complex future is no longer one of uncertainty and fear, but of hope and joyful expectation. Christians live with the conviction that the end of history will bring nothing but the fulfilment of the hope of seeing the teacher again and the satisfaction of being welcomed by him with the same openness and desire to be together forever. Authentic disciples are connected to the life and teaching of the master and make the effort to actualize them at all times, even when the world seems to be falling apart. They do not abandon their mission and do not give up their status even when things seem to be out of control.

Last but not least, the disciples are advised to be watchful and prayerful (Mark 13:33) – to remain always in a deep relationship with God and in a continuous discipline of evaluating their own lives and what is happening around them. In a short parable, the master likens the disciples to servants to whom the departed master delegates the authority to take care of his house. There is the promise of the master's return, but no details as to when he will arrive. The task of the servants is to concern themselves with the management of the estate, not with finding out when the departed one will return. In order that the attention and conscience of the disciples may remain awake, and that their action may focus on what has been entrusted to them, the master has left them the useful aid of prayer. The teacher encourages the disciples to be watchful, that is, to be like a living and working presence, aware of responsibilities, risks, and dangers. Prayer is the most effective way to maintain this state of watchfulness and keen discernment. Mission in the world is exercised by keeping constantly in mind the certainty of the return of the master and the end of all things. This hope must sustain the life and mission of the disciples, keep them on their feet in difficult moments, and guard them from any temptation to abandon their vocation. The eschatological reference does not necessarily determine an orientation towards the future, but a focus on the seriousness of the fulfilment of the mission, on the quality of the disciple's authentic witness in this world. Prayer supports this effort to focus on the actuality, strengthens the attention to the real issues, and helps the disciple to remain awake and articulate in the face of daily challenges. Prayer is also a way of constantly affirming dependence on God and assuming mission in the world as a partnership with the Holy Spirit. Through the ongoing practice of prayer, disciples exercise their capacity to understand God's will, to discern the logic of his economy in the world, and to understand the role of believers in the context in which they have been placed.

The reception of disciples into the world depends a great deal on both the quality of their ministry and the context in which they operate. The teacher does not invite disciples to seek conflict with people but warns them that the world will resist their message and association with his person. There is also a risk that disciples will misunderstand people's reactions and see themselves as persecuted when this is not the case. The rejection or distance that may result from the Christian offer should not always be understood as hostility and persecution. Genuine discipleship is based on a fundamental respect for human freedom to decide on Christ's invitation and willingness to follow his way. Equally, it is important to stress that those who are disciples of Jesus and have chosen to bear his name in history will have to struggle with the reality of evil and sin manifested in various forms. The way of Christ does not admit accommodation and dilution of the identity received, but requires its manifestation with vigour and discernment in any socio-historical context, regardless of the position adopted by political and religious authorities, regardless of the attitude of the recipients of their ministry.

Questions

1. What are the main elements of your own cultural and social context that challenge or put to the test your identity as a disciple of Jesus?

2. What is the meaning of Christ's message that the world will always hate us because of his name?

3. What is your calling or mission as a disciple of Jesus where you have been placed?

4. Are there unclear or insufficiently assumed elements in your own Christian identity that amplify the tension of your relationship with the spirit of this world?

5. In a society where most people declare themselves Christians, how can we affirm our discipleship to Jesus and carry forward his mission in the world?

15

Dealing with Falls

The most delicate moments in our lives are those when we are put to the test. Faith or fidelity, virtues or hopes can be stretched to the limit and can force us to make decisions in highly tense contexts, in relation to critical situations and crucial objectives. The tests in a person's life are an opportunity for deep self-knowledge, for assessing who we really are, for checking what we can achieve. The importance of the tests is revealed not only in our ability to pass them well, but also in the way we know how to handle our failures – the times when we fail as disciples in the trials of life. These moments can come upon us at times when we least expect them; at other times they can be part of a training strategy, of a path that someone has planned. Divine pedagogy, along with that which we humans employ in society, frequently employs assessment or testing to strengthen our personalities and to determine progress, know our limits, and overcome obstacles.

From the Gospel, we see that Jesus frequently practiced this strategy of evaluating his disciples, both as a method of preparation for future steps in the process and as a way of personal analysis. But in the final week of Jesus's mission, we are almost at the end of the road, and we probably expect the master to draw the line and give the disciples the final examination. Things don't happen that way, because the end of the process has the teacher at its centre, not the followers. In the last week of Christ's ministry in the world, the disciples will quickly enter into a hard school of evaluation, without the events that happen being explicitly foreseen by the master. We are witnessing the moment when both the mission and the personality of Jesus are called into question by the political and religious authorities. In this context, the condition of the one who associates with Jesus – the disciple – is also threatened. The most important challenge seems to be related to how disciples remain faithful to the master, his values and his way of life. Even though the situation at the time was unique and the context very special, the lessons experienced by the disciples and the extreme situations of this kind have been replayed again and again throughout time until today.

After an inventory of warnings and exhortations about the future, Jesus turns his attention to the final part of his mission. The disciples witness a series of events with profound implications, and their participation oscillates and is frequently meaningless. An early picture presented by Mark is of the house of Simon the Leper, shortly before the Passover celebration (Mark 14:3–9). Two important points are underlined by the biblical text regarding the disciples. The first records their reaction to the exceptional gesture of the woman who anointed Jesus's body with myrrh. For today's reader, this pragmatic positioning of the disciples in the face of the apparent waste of precious goods is scandalous. They display no reflex of appreciation or astonishment, no trace of admiration for an act of great appreciation towards their master, no sign of consideration for the one who had discipled them and brought them through so many extraordinary experiences. One may wonder where this attitude of the disciples, who only consider the gesture waste at the expense of the poor, comes from? Is that all they were able to do after what they learned from Jesus throughout their training? Are they left with a social theology that no longer has a sense of generosity or sensitivity to profound gestures?

This reaction seems to set the ground for the second important point made in the biblical text concerning the disciples, as it records the most dishonourable act that could happen among them. In a moment of blindness and foolishness, one of the Twelve goes to sell the teacher to the religious authorities. The gesture of betrayal seems to come as a continuation of a state of lethargy that gives way to a collective protest against the woman who anoints Jesus's body. We can speculate and wonder about Judas' personality and his propensity for petty gain, but the betrayal of the teacher cannot be attributed to him alone. The rift in the small community of disciples must be looked at more deeply. We recall, in passing, the disciples' lack of understanding of what Jesus announced would happen in Jerusalem, and their focus on very mundane issues of who would be greater after the teacher's departure. It seems pretty clear that the disciples were not experiencing events as intensely as Jesus, and that their attention was elsewhere. Although Jesus's message of vigilance and the danger of deception and false redemptive projects is still heard in the background, the disciples are relaxed and living in the inertia of those still immature and under the protective hand of their mentor. Events take them by surprise, facts flow in a different logic than expected, and errors are made one after another.

The next dense scene in the biblical text is the Feast of Unleavened Bread (Mark 14:12–25). Following Jewish tradition, Jesus gathers with his twelve disciples to celebrate the Passover. As with the entry into Jerusalem, the disciples witness a scene that shows that the teacher knows the way he must go as he follows God's plan. But what happens at the table seems to reinforce the idea that the disciples are experiencing things on a different level. Two points are strongly emphasized in Mark's Gospel, and the attitude of the disciples suggests that they face new challenges which they fail lamentably. First comes the shocking statement in which Jesus announces that one of the twelve is a traitor who is selling out his teacher. It is hard to say how the disciples should or could have been expected to react. But what the biblical text emphasizes seems more like a gesture of resignation. Everyone wonders if it is him and grieves. That's all. Nothing more. It seems outrageous to accept a truth and do nothing, to try nothing, even though you may not be able to change much. The gesture matters, the attitude speaks to one's state of spirit, maturity, and alertness. The biblical text tells us that the Passover meal and ritual continued as if nothing had happened, as if Jesus had simply made a casual announcement. It is in this setting that the second situation of great tension is recorded, which the disciples completely miss. The master makes an important change, redirecting the dynamics of the Jewish celebration, without seeing any reaction from the participants. In the context of the breaking of the bread and the blessing of the cup, Jesus gives new meaning to the whole celebration and links it to himself, to his body, and to his death. Although what Jesus says is a scandal to the mind, a completely irrational invitation to eat his body and drink his blood, the reaction of the disciples is flat, like that of an anesthetized audience watching in complete silence. Only at the end, when Jesus explicitly tells them that they will all leave him because they will be scandalized by him, does the reaction of Peter and then the others appear, pledging that they will not leave their teacher. But their promises do not seem convincing. Jesus insists and repeats the idea, at which point Peter becomes upset and challenged by his statements.

The third scene that catches our attention is the one in the Garden of Gethsemane (14:32–42). It is a moment of maximum tension for Jesus and of a disarming and overwhelming numbness for the disciples. Explicitly, for the first time in the discipleship relationship, the master shows himself vulnerable. The text insists on and retells details of Jesus's state of being. Importantly, the teacher shares his feelings and experiences and expects the disciples to assist and support him. Yes, for the first time we see Jesus saying that he needs support from the disciples and asks them to pray with him, to watch with him. Clearly, we cannot grasp the scale of the situation and the burden of the moment. We are also tempted to agree with the disciples and rather understand their state of lassitude and tiredness, the fact that they could not keep vigil and fell prey to sleep. But we cannot overlook the fact that the master had expectations of them, relied on their support, and wanted their company and assistance. Three times he came to see if they were with him, if they were watching and praying, and each time he found them sleeping. It is so sad not to find support when you need it, to be left alone by those close to you, and to find that your pain is not shared by those close to you at the hardest time of your life. This is how Jesus's discipleship relationship with his disciples seems to end. It seems like a great failure, a painful end to a long journey full of beautiful experiences. After Jesus overcomes the moment of his own struggle and takes it upon himself to go all the way, the picture changes. Left alone in his mission, the teacher is apprehended, and the disciples wake up and run for their lives. They all flee and leave him, after a brief attempt by one to defend him with a sword.

A final picture relevant to the behaviour of the disciples is after Jesus's capture and the whole trajectory related to his trial and crucifixion (Mark 14:43–72). The disciples probably still experience great shock at seeing their master bound and taken by soldiers before the authorities. We don't know if they have had time to reflect on their reaction and the cowardice with which they have abandoned their teacher at this moment of crisis. But the biblical text insists on giving Peter, the leader of the disciples, a strong and temperamental personality. Although he has sworn that he is ready to give his life for Jesus, Simon the fisherman ends up fulfilling his teacher's prophecy that he will deny him three times before dawn. These things do happen, but that's not the point; it is not about the correctness of Jesus's prediction, but much more than that, it is about an important lesson. It is clear that in the end Peter realizes his own failure and unwise zeal. This hot-tempered man's weeping can mean a lot. But what could he do better? At least he tried, he had the courage to declare his intentions, to express his personality, even if he then failed and did not translate things into action. The question arises whether the disciples were still immature, and the process of discipleship ended prematurely, somewhat forcibly. Or perhaps the last lesson is the one they have to go through, to taste the bitterness of the fall, the pain of helplessness and failure, the disappointment of not knowing themselves well enough and thinking too highly of themselves.

With this final episode, the Twelve exit the scene, and Jesus is left to carry his destiny to the end. The Gospel of Mark tells us that all the disciples have left Jesus (Mark 14:50). The master is tried, convicted, and the sentence is quickly carried out. After the authorities are assured that he is dead, he is allowed to be buried with the support of a rich man named Joseph. Despite this grim picture, the end of the discipleship process does not remain in dark colours. On the one hand, the biblical text tells us that there were several women who accompanied Jesus from Galilee. We are given the names of three of them: Mary Magdalene, Mary the mother of Jesus, and Salome. The text also says that there were other women who came to Jerusalem with the teacher, and they were all watching the crucifixion from afar. They remain faithful to the teacher and are with him to the end, witnessing Jesus's death and burial, just as they witnessed his entire mission begun in Galilee and now completed in Jerusalem (Mark 15:40–41). Even if the biblical text does not give these women the title of disciples, they have more than earned it and should be regarded with great admiration and willingness to learn from their experience with Jesus.

On the other hand, another type of disciple surprisingly appears from afar, a man who was waiting for the kingdom of God and who lived according to the logic of what the teacher preached (Mark 16:42–47). Joseph of Arimathea, a leader of the Jewish people, is less traumatized by what happened and makes a beautiful gesture for the master. His social position allows him to do so, and he intervenes with the authorities with a request to take Jesus's body and bury it. Mark says nothing about Jesus's other disciples (a larger circle of disciples is mentioned at the beginning, from whom he chose the Twelve), but we suspect that they too witnessed what happened in Jerusalem helplessly, from near and far. The final word, however, goes to the stone, which closes everything and leaves the disciples without a teacher, but with a legacy, with a mission to carry out in the world, with an identity built with him and to be affirmed.

While we might be tempted to judge the disciples harshly for their chain of failures in such a short period of time, and think what a tremendous opportunity they had to live alongside the great master of history, nevertheless things should not be judged simplistically. Failures are part of our limited experience. They are part of the normality of life, including that of faith. The evaluation of failures must always be done in context and in relation to the dynamics of the discipleship process. The important thing here is the lessons we learn whenever we fall, the seriousness with which we try to overcome our failures, the attitude with which we relate to others who go through the same experiences as we do. Perhaps it is less about moral performance and achievement than it is about aspirations and the attitude with which we rise above our falls, the hope of what we can become and what we can achieve at every stage of life as disciples of the great teacher Jesus Christ. It is crucially important to observe the realism and honesty with which the biblical text presents the disciples' experience, and the seriousness with which not only the achievements but also the failures are addressed. Jesus alerted the disciples and warned them of dangers and pitfalls, and of the limits of human experience in the world. But the teacher never passed judgement on their lives or asked them for more than they could bear. On the contrary, he trusted in their ability to continue their mission, to overcome problems and their own failures, and he always believed in their power to change through the values of faith and the aspirations of a consistent life based on their relationship with God and the model of their teacher.

The failures of Jesus's followers, then, are also our failures throughout Christian history. All this shows us that we are on the way and that discipleship is never over. What happened to the Twelve is not a failure that ends everything within the boundaries of human weakness and powerlessness. The failures of the disciples pale before the strength with which the master took on the human condition and walked the path to the end. His sacrifice is the foundation on which the disciples can rise and follow his path. Discipleship is based on what Christ has achieved and on his continued presence with his followers in the world. We cannot remain disappointed by the disciples' reaction in the teacher's most difficult moments. Their lesson shows us the profound need for change in human nature and the stakes of Jesus's ministry. What matters is that the master had the courage and strength to accomplish what was entrusted to him and that he did not abandon his disciples. Discipleship continues in the world because the teacher has succeeded and so the possibility remains for his followers to be healed. Weeping and the bitter taste of failure are part of the discipleship process, part of the dynamics of human transformation. Despite their failures, believers have the chance to get up and lean on God's outstretched hand.

Questions

1. How do you understand the role of failure and its effects in the discipleship process?

2. What cultural and contextual elements contribute to a negative or judgemental attitude towards those who have had failures on their path of faith?

3. How do you react to your own failures? What about those of others?

4. What are the main problematic issues in the way of dealing with those who make mistakes, including major ones, in the Christian community of which you are a part, as well as in the discipleship relationships you know?

5. In what ways can the Christian community support or protect people involved in discipleship relationships who experience various forms of failure?

16

Sending Disciples into the World

The betrayal, suffering and death of the teacher must have been felt as a great failure by the disciples. Although they were warned that these things would happen, it all seems meaningless in relation to the mission of proclaiming the gospel and preparing for the establishment of the kingdom of God. Moreover, precisely because Jesus also prophesied the disciples' flight and abandonment of their master, the scenario becomes more grim, more dramatic. Is this a form of determinism? Could the disciples have overcome their fear and stood firm with Jesus in his most difficult moments? Or did the human condition allow for no more than that? The Gospel of Mark does not mention details of what followed, the disciples' experiences, or any analysis of what happened. It all develops extremely quickly and events move towards the teacher's tragic end. If he had such an end to his life, what would happen to the disciples? Will they be able to regroup, to reconsider their ministry and vocation? To make things even more complicated, in the last chapter of the Gospel, Mark shows us the scene of the women going to the tomb to anoint Jesus's body, according to the Jewish tradition (Mark 16:1–8). As they arrive at the tomb of the teacher, they are surprised by some totally unexpected things: the stone that enclosed the cave had been thrown aside; inside they find a young man dressed in white, and Jesus's body is missing; they receive a strange message that Jesus has risen and is no longer there; they are sent to tell the disciples about the resurrection and that they will meet Jesus in Galilee; it is pointed out that all this had already been announced by the teacher beforehand and that things should not surprise the disciples. At this scene, which is seemingly from another world, the natural reaction of the women is one of astonishment and fear. The biblical text tells us that they fled from the tomb and said nothing to anyone, being overcome with trembling and bewilderment. What, after all, produced all this tension in the women? Was it the disturbing presence of the angel? Is it inconceivable that the master's body has disappeared and that a whole conspiracy may be behind it? Were they tricked and sent from there not to ask questions? Did their great grief at the loss of Jesus contribute to this also?

The message and the reality of Jesus's resurrection were then, and still are today, realities that are difficult for the human mind and heart to accept. The realism with which the Gospel presents Jesus's traumatic end is unequivocal. He was swallowed up in death, he received the punishment required by the law, he left our world as an outcast. To the common mind, the women in the group of followers and his disciples, having seen their plans destroyed, must have made up this story of his resurrection. It was the only way to salvage the situation, to give some kind of continuity to their dream of greatness in the future kingdom of God. As Mark the Evangelist presents things to us, the women had a vision of a young man dressed in white. They did not meet Jesus and had rather a traumatic experience. They were frightened and fled from the tomb and were left with this mysterious experience, open to interpretation. This is how the end of the story of Jesus and his disciples can be understood. The Gospel of Mark offers no evidence or proof of the resurrection. We have the word of a man appearing in a vision and the word of women frightened and traumatized by the death of the teacher and his disappearance from the tomb. In the two older manuscripts that preserve the text of this Gospel, this is how things end, with the eighth verse. Jesus does not show himself; only the promise of meeting his disciples in Galilee remains. In other later manuscripts, there is another part that ends the text of this Gospel and records first the episode in which Jesus shows himself to one of the women seeking his body, and then the one in which Christ introduces himself to the other disciples. We leave aside the technical discussion of manuscripts and the question of possible later intervention on the text. It is important to consider the message of this text. For the theme of discipleship, in this section we have an illuminating conclusion and a final challenge to Jesus's disciples.

The text repeats the mention of women, these interesting and eager disciples, and tells us that Jesus shows himself to Mary Magdalene (Mark 16:9–14). In the characteristic style of Mark, everything happens in a hurry, without details, without any dialogue between the two. We can suspect that the author is suggesting that we pay attention to what follows and that Jesus intends to set a new challenge for the disciples. We may wonder why Jesus does not show himself directly to all the disciples, and why this strategy of sending a messenger first is needed. We begin to understand the master's intention when we consider the state of the disciples and their reaction to the words of the one who visited his tomb. We are faced here with a new test devised by this original master. When things are at their worst, when the disciples are weeping and wailing (Mark 16:10), it seems that the teacher is playing tricks and sending them strange messages. This process of preparing the disciples for their encounter with Jesus can be understood in the logic of the master's discipleship strategy. Although we would have liked the proof of the resurrection to come immediately and directly, things build up differently. Even if he is absent, the teacher makes his presence felt through his style of working, through the way he approaches his disciples. Discipleship is not over and it seems that it will never end.

Although the teacher is away, the lessons continue. Even if to some this tactic of not relaxing at all the conditions of the troubled and disoriented apprentices seems unfair, things are slowly moving towards clarification. But it is precisely in this sensitive and seemingly hopeless state that the master's way of working remains constructive. This is his style, coming up with challenges and support for the disciples in their state of difficulty. When those who remained in Jerusalem first heard the message of the resurrection, most of the disciples, including the eleven apostles, did not believe it. They were too hardened by grief and sorrow, too scarred by the horror of the events. A second resurrection message follows, brought by two of the disciples who meet Jesus on the road. Even this time the eleven who remain faithful to the master are unable to believe, to accept that Jesus has risen from the grave, that he has risen from the dead. Finally, the teacher shows himself to the apostles as they sit at the table. Presumably, they were now ready for this meeting. Again, the biblical text surprises us and gives no details of the disciples' reaction. We have only a brief record of Jesus rebuking them for not believing the messages of those who saw him resurrected. This remark is very important with regard to the last lesson the disciples are exposed to in the presence of the master: Jesus does not rebuke them for not believing in him, in the words he spoke before his passion, but rather for not believing in the message of their fellow disciples. This new emphasis becomes significant in view of the mission to come, of the disciples' life in the world as messengers of the teacher, servants of God who carry forward the work of Jesus Christ. The mission of the teacher will continue in history on the basis of this witness of the disciples about who Jesus is and what he has done, about the call of all people to become his disciples and to follow his model of life.

The concluding section of the Gospel is the teacher's last message before leaving the world (Mark 16:15–20). Essentially, Jesus reiterates the theme of sending disciples into the world in order to proclaim the gospel to all. The last lesson they witness is important for what was going to follow. The disciples' mission is to carry forward what they have received from the teacher, and people are invited to believe based on their word. In this sensitive lesson, at a very delicate moment, the teacher insists on the ability of the disciples to believe as a result of the witness of their fellows. This change in the process of discipleship could for some be a change of meaning, that places everything that follows from here on in the category of second-class activities. The Twelve, along with the other disciples, received the gospel directly from Jesus, and the rest of the people are to receive it from his disciples. This seems like an important and perhaps difficult change for the reader of the Gospel to accept. However, if we look at things carefully, Jesus's message emphasizes that the basis of the process continues to be faith, the capacity of the human being to be open and to receive the gospel message, no matter which way it is transmitted. Jesus's contemporaries faced the same challenge of relating to Jesus by faith, and their task is to ask people to believe not in themselves but in the one who sent them and in his message. It should also be stressed that disciples are not mere neutral instruments of communication. Their lives, the way they actualize the values of Jesus, and the transparency of their transformation process are as important as the message they speak. From this perspective, there is no advantage either for the disciples sent by Jesus into the world, or for the later disciples who are invited to receive the gospel through the mission of the former. To reinforce this idea, the biblical text highlights at least two key points.

First of all, the focus is on the faith of the person, on the free response to the gospel message. The same mechanism worked for those who were with Jesus during his mission to the world. As we have observed throughout the Gospel of Mark, the school of discipleship had the goal of awakening and developing the disciples' faith. On this basis, the relationship with Jesus and his mission was not carried out according to the logic of the world, but according to that of God's wisdom. The discipleship process leads to this culmination of the maturity of faith, of the capacity to receive the word of Jesus from his disciples, of the readiness to accept the message and mission of the gospel from those who follow Christ. If the continuity of the teacher's work in the world depends on this crucial aspect, it means that the discipleship process is also crucial. Jesus left behind a group of disciples who learned this profound lesson. The fulfilment of the mandate they received requires such an investment in others. Disciple-making is the essential engine of the community established by the Son of God in history, not just an aspect of the cultural and religious context of the time in which Jesus lived. The gospel reaches people because there are disciples, people who were willing to go through this process of transforming their being and embracing the values left by Christ. And genuine disciples produce spiritual growth in others: they help to develop and mature faith in others, that is, they make other disciples.

Second, disciples are sent out into the world to carry on the mission of Jesus with a clear empowerment or mandate from the master. Disciples receive authority from their teacher to be able to carry out what they have been entrusted with and to accompany their message with the signs they have seen in Jesus. In other words, the physical absence of the master does not mark a significant change in the nature and dynamics of his ministry in the world. On the contrary, the master remains present with his disciples through this perpetual transmission of his authority from one generation to the next, through the fulfilment of his words in those who believe in him. The vocation of the disciples is to present their teacher to the world; that is, their life is to show him, to make visible the one they believe in and follow. The dynamic of discipleship in history involves this twofold effort: the desire to become like Christ, our model, and the investment in helping others grow in the same direction – participating in the discipleship of others.

The Christian tradition records an enormous amount of discussions on the Gospel text dealing with the signs of Jesus's authority in the world in the context of the mission entrusted to the disciples. In the spirit of the biblical text, the emphasis is not on the existence of a concrete number of signs that must be repeated over and over again, but on the idea of the existence of such a manifestation of the authority of Jesus Christ. Signs have the function of indicating the reality of God's presence; they have value because they convey a powerful message for a particular context and therefore have a particular character. The biblical text concludes with the phrase which underlines God's presence with the disciples, an assistance which gives them authority, a manifest guidance which accompanies the disciples' mission with signs. But it must be stressed that in this regard the text of Scripture is very clear: it is important for the disciples to fulfil their mission, while the appearance and manifestation of signs is God's responsibility. Their absence does not necessarily mean that the disciples are not fulfilling their mission properly. Signs are not an expression of divine economy confirming disciples' performance or maturity. Rather they depend on God's decision to manifest his presence in one way or another to people and thus confirm the identity and ministry of his disciples. It remains for the disciple to take his role seriously and to believe in the continuing manifest presence of Jesus Christ in the world with his own.

The Gospel ends with this picture: Jesus is lifted up to heaven, to the right hand of God, that is, to a position of authority and glory; and the disciples are invested to continue his mission in the world accompanied by his presence, by God's concrete and authoritative assistance (Mark 16:19–20). This picture has been growing ever wider in history since then, and it applies to us today. But what gives unity to this whole is the theme of discipleship. We cannot neglect what Jesus did and what he has left as a legacy to his disciples. He did not establish a religion or an institutional structure, but neither did he condemn such constructions. The core of his mission was to bring the gospel message to the world and to fulfil it first in his own life. He also found the best way and the most effective strategy for his work to reach people, namely to plant in others what he lived. Discipleship is a way of life, a process by which humanity's being is transformed and takes on more and more the outline of the model – which is Jesus Christ. The teacher came into the world precisely for this purpose, to be the engine of a new way of life, to bring change and renewal to the human being and to restore it to a normal relationship with God. What Jesus achieved is accessible to us and can be achieved if we are open to follow his path, that is, to be his disciples and to walk the path of discipleship. History bears witness to this and shows us that it can be done. Jesus's message and his way of life have been passed on. The mandate of discipleship is not over yet, and continues until the end of history. For every apprentice, discipleship is a lifelong process and a path that cannot be abandoned without the risk of losing faith and purpose. Fortunately, there are disciples who follow Jesus, and God's presence in the world accompanies them in the most unexpected ways and signs. Faith is a living reality that gives courage and determination to those who wish to become like their Lord and teacher Jesus Christ.

Questions

1. How is the process of sending people out for ministry understood in the context of Christianity today? Sent by whom, where, for what purpose?

2. In what ways does being sent as a disciple take into account our profession, family and civic responsibilities?

3. How do we understand the Great Commission of disciples to "all nations" in the context of the society in which we live?

4. What are the ways in which we fulfil this command of Christ?

5. In what way is the quality of our identity as disciples of the Lord expressed in this process?

6. How is the Great Commission translated into practice in the local Christian community in which you worship?

Conclusion

The theme of discipleship is of pressing relevance not only to Christian communities but to all areas of activity in society. The increasing complexity of the reality of life and the ever-increasing rate of change make continuous learning, discipline, and the need for sustained support a priority in the process of the permanent transformation of living conditions, from professional to social, religious, and cultural. The value of mentoring is being recognized on many levels of today's society, and this practice is being taken seriously in companies, universities, and other organizations. The benefits of apprenticeship for various activities and for specific periods of time are already known and are the subject of seminars and books on the importance of mentor-assisted training.

It is increasingly clear that progress in one's career or spiritual life depends significantly on the use of discipleship. In the places where this pedagogical strategy is practised, the basic vision is that each person being discipled must become able and willing to train others in turn. This is how values, skills, and ideas are best transmitted. The requirements are different from one field to another, but the fundamental rule is that everything depends on the difference in potential between people. When individuals have more of something than one of their peers, when they have greater skills and a certain amount of knowledge, then they can play the role of a mentor, and it is important to understand that they can help the other person. Sometimes the practice is institutionalized and becomes a professional obligation or part of one's responsibility in the organizational context in which they find themselves. Frequently, for some people, such things are done voluntarily as a matter of conscience, out of a desire to contribute to the development of an idea, project, or people.

For Christian communities, recovering the value of discipleship and practising it as a normal part of the life of faith is a necessity. As many voices of prominent Christian leaders today point out, the future will bring substantial changes to the dynamics of local church life. The trend of de-confessionalization, the loss of importance of the ecclesial institution, globalization and multiculturalism are all factors that force us to evaluate and find strategies for the development of Christian communities in order to remain alive, prophetic, and impactful for people. No matter how local churches are reconfigured, discipleship cannot be missing from the fundamental toolkit. The diversification of the needs of Christians, and the presence of local and regional differences, can only be addressed in Christian ministry by focusing mission on the fundamentals of the life of faith, staying as close as possible to each person and their specific problems. The era of large churches and the presentation of the gospel through evangelistic campaigns that gather large crowds of people seem to have passed. Even in small local churches, the purpose of public meetings can no longer go beyond the liturgical and sacramental function. The complexity of people's needs demands that the faithful be oriented towards their fellow human beings, either through actions and strategies well defined in context, or through less systematized approaches, but with the vision of engaging people in relationships of discipleship.

Scripture establishes an equivalence between being a Christian and being a disciple (Acts 11:26). Discipleship involves being a follower of Jesus Christ, accepting him as Lord and teacher, and master in all things. This leads to keeping his commandments, walking in his way, and transforming our being according to his standards. Christian discipleship is a way of life, an experience that affects all dimensions of life. It is the experience of a journey, the adventure of humanity's return to God together with the whole world.

The Gospel of Mark has allowed us to discover some useful aspects for a better understanding of Christian discipleship. We do not have a recipe or steps to follow to become disciples of Jesus Christ. Rather, through the biblical text we witness the presentation of a real experience that took place in history. Moreover, it is presented to us by a biblical author who himself went through the school of discipleship as a disciple of one of the twelve apostles. As far as I have been able, I have highlighted a number of features of the people involved in the process, aspects that give colour and intensity, which can be considered ingredients of the relationship between the teacher and his followers. Among others, I noticed: the openness and authenticity of the teacher; the way in which he was able to see the profile and traits of each disciple and then to stimulate, confront or shape them; the importance of Jesus's working strategy, namely the concrete participation of the disciples in the teacher's mission, the exposure to teachings in public and their refinement in private, the submission to evaluations and tests, etc.; the idea that discipleship is not an end in itself, but a process of transformation, of assuming a new identity capable of carrying forward the mission of the teacher; that discipleship is not a path accessible to or dedicated to an elite (cultural, ethnic, religious or gender-wise), but a personal experience to which anyone is invited at any time; the importance of the work of preparing disciples for the period of separation from the teacher and the warnings about the condition of the disciple in the world; the ability of disciples to become disciple-makers themselves; and a paradigm of discipleship that is closely linked to our nature as relational beings subject to becoming, that is the way God uses to grow us and bring us to himself.

We hope that this text will be a useful guide for readers in supporting their efforts to read Mark's Gospel and to understand what Jesus did with his disciples. It would be desirable that the reading of this text and the things assimilated could be shared with others and then lived out in one's own discipleship relationships. Last but not least, we hope that what is presented here will be a real encouragement to carry forward what Jesus Christ left us all as a legacy, to "make disciples of all nations."

May God help us!

Questions

1. What are your main conclusions on the theme of discipleship at the end of the reading of this book?

2. What helped you most in this book?

3. Do you know people who want to become disciples of others but can't find a mentor? What are the main reasons for this?

4. How would you encourage someone to become a disciple, that is, to enter into a formative relationship with a more mature Christian?

5. Can you be a mentor to others if you haven't had a mentor yourself or if you don't give an account of your life to someone in particular?

6. What is the price you are willing to pay in order to be able to mentor others?

7. What do you need in your own spiritual life to be able to disciple others?

8. To what extent do you think it is legitimate and possible for someone to have multiple mentors for different periods or well-defined objectives?

9. How do you understand the idea of a time horizon for the next stage of the Christian life?

10. As a mentor or disciple, can you outline what would be the most important components of your own Christian life project for the next 5–10 years?

Afterword

For a reader, a book is like a window which, if opened, widens the horizon of knowledge. For authors, their creation is the legacy they leave to their readers. In itself, the book is an invitation from the author to the reader, marking the path that they both travel in order to meet somehow. Authors make themselves available and vulnerable, initiating the dialogue through an intimate exposition of their thoughts. Readers respond to the author's intention, giving voice and personal meaning to the message received. However, in the context of this conversation, the two rarely have the chance to get to know their interlocutor.

Within the Christian Reading and Dialogue Group of Iași, Romania, the meeting between these two actors – writer and reader – was made possible through the reading of the manuscript that later materialized in this book, *Called to Discipleship*. We had the chance to sit down at the dialogue table with the author himself, in order to debate the ideas that captivated us, opened our eyes or sometimes confused us. . We asked questions and received answers that brought us new understandings on the theme of discipleship or that threw us back into the arena of inner turmoil, in the struggle with new questions and the search for new clarifications. However, such an outcome is normal and to be expected in the process of growth, and the interaction with such a text provided us with guidance rather than solutions, called us to an uncomfortable effort to recognize and overcome our limits, to tread the hard path of knowledge, and did not allow us to remain anchored in rigid structures, or to be persuaded by flat or restrictive discourses.

From the very first pages of this analysis of the Gospel text, we entered, together with the author, into an adventure which profoundly changed our lives, as was the case of the first disciples who, invited by their master Jesus, opened themselves to a total transformation of their lives. Discipleship seen as a vocation invites Christians to reconsider their identity beyond a religious system, by engaging in a living relationship of discipleship to the master par excellence, who is Christ.

The author invites us to walk with the first disciples in their formation process as presented to us by Mark the Evangelist, but we are often challenged to think outside the theological framework we are used to. The text abounds with profound reflections that spring from an overt contemplation of points of view different from those commonly heard in church, yet worthy of being extracted as aphorisms and foundations of discipleship or of the life of faith in general. Based on a personalist view of the analysis of the biblical text, inspired by patristic theology, the author offers the reader a different kind of interpretation, much more rooted in the thinking of the first centuries; we are dealing with a much more human Jesus, with much simpler disciples, who are not idealized, but are marked by all kinds of failures, as well as successes. This way of feeling the master and his disciples at every step is delightful for the readers and helps them identify with the apostles of Jesus.

At times, the author even proposes certain hypotheses which, although at first sight they may be scandalous, have the didactic role of arousing our curiosity and moving us from our fixations. The text itself does not set out to be "tamed," to present the ideas as in a systematic theology manual, but rather engages the readers in the story, in a living journey; it does not spare them, but throws them into the same circle of questions and anxieties that the disciples went through, in the hope that the same adherence to the master's teaching and life will occur.

We have tended to read the text in the grid of inter-human discipleship, but the author has helped us to understand that, in essence, every Christian is first and foremost a disciple of Jesus invited to live according to his model of life. All the lessons we learn from the life of the disciples we must fundamentally take on board in relationship with Jesus. Only afterwards it is possible to follow discipleship relationships with people, which also have their role.

Given that in most of contemporary Christianity there are no direct discipleship relationships between people based on this Christlike model, the author's invitation to engage us - readers from different denominational backgrounds - by giving an initial feedback - was like a taste of normality - which should characterize the life of faith.

Our book club aims to be an adequate framework for apprenticeship through an intellectual formative process (but not only that), which contributes to the development of analytical and critical thinking, which helps to discover working tools, be they theological, philosophical, psychological, or other, and to discover a way of operating with them in the work of understanding the foundations of Christian teaching. Within this framework, approaching the Scriptures with a teacher like the author of this book was a valuable opportunity to lay new bricks at the foundation of our Christian life.

The approach proposed by the author, to explore the foundations of discipleship in the model of Jesus with the apostles and to build the Christian identity on the basis of discipleship, transcends the boundaries of this book, even confessionalism itself, uniting in an ecumenical way the whole of Christianity. It is the duty of each generation to update the foundations of Christian discipleship in its own context, assuming them in a communitarian spirit.

It is our hope that such an understanding of the calling to discipleship will spread and will live through the ages until we meet our Lord and Master Jesus Christ and all his disciples.

The members of the Christian Reading and
Dialogue Group of Iaşi, Romania
7 May 2019

References

Bayer, H.F. *A Theology of Mark: The Dynamic Between Christology and Authentic Discipleship.* New Jersey: P&R Publishing, 2012.

Best, E. *Following Jesus: Discipleship in the Gospel of Mark.* Edinburgh: T&T Clark, 1981.

Bjorg, D.E. *Every Believer a Disciple.* Carlisle: Langham Global Library, 2015.

Bonhoeffer, D. *The Cost of Discipleship.* New York: Touchstone, 1995.

Burggraff, A.T. *Discipleship in the Early Church.* Wapwallopen: Shepherds Press, 2022.

Edwards, J.R. *The Gospel According to Mark.* Grand Rapids: Eerdmans, 2001.

France, R.T. *The Gospel of Mark.* Grand Rapids: Eerdmans 2002.

Johnson, K.L. *Theology as Discipleship.* Downers Grove: IVP Academic 2015.

Meitzner Yoder, L.S., ed. *Living Radical Discipleship.* Carlisle: Langham Global Library, 2021.

Ortiz, J.C. *Disciple.* Lake Mary: Charisma House 1996.

Painter, J. *Mark's Gospel.* London: Routledge, 1997.

Stott, J. *The Radical Disciple: Some Neglected Aspects of Our Calling.* Downers Grove: IVP Books, 2014.

Vandebeulque, D. *Douze hommes ordinaires.* Marne-la-Vallée: Farel, 2006.

Wright, N.T. *Following Jesus: Biblical Reflections on Discipleship.* Grand Rapids: Eerdmans 2014.

Langham Literature and its imprints are a ministry of Langham Partnership.

Langham Partnership is a global fellowship working in pursuit of the vision God entrusted to its founder John Stott –

to facilitate the growth of the church in maturity and Christ-likeness through raising the standards of biblical preaching and teaching.

Our vision is to see churches in the Majority World equipped for mission and growing to maturity in Christ through the ministry of pastors and leaders who believe, teach and live by the word of God.

Our mission is to strengthen the ministry of the word of God through:
- nurturing national movements for biblical preaching
- fostering the creation and distribution of evangelical literature
- enhancing evangelical theological education

especially in countries where churches are under-resourced.

Our ministry

Langham Preaching partners with national leaders to nurture indigenous biblical preaching movements for pastors and lay preachers all around the world. With the support of a team of trainers from many countries, a multi-level programme of seminars provides practical training, and is followed by a programme for training local facilitators. Local preachers' groups and national and regional networks ensure continuity and ongoing development, seeking to build vigorous movements committed to Bible exposition.

Langham Literature provides Majority World preachers, scholars and seminary libraries with evangelical books and electronic resources through publishing and distribution, grants and discounts. The programme also fosters the creation of indigenous evangelical books in many languages, through writer's grants, strengthening local evangelical publishing houses, and investment in major regional literature projects, such as one volume Bible commentaries like *The Africa Bible Commentary* and *The South Asia Bible Commentary*.

Langham Scholars provides financial support for evangelical doctoral students from the Majority World so that, when they return home, they may train pastors and other Christian leaders with sound, biblical and theological teaching. This programme equips those who equip others. Langham Scholars also works in partnership with Majority World seminaries in strengthening evangelical theological education. A growing number of Langham Scholars study in high quality doctoral programmes in the Majority World itself. As well as teaching the next generation of pastors, graduated Langham Scholars exercise significant influence through their writing and leadership.

To learn more about Langham Partnership and the work we do visit **langham.org**

Milton Keynes UK
Ingram Content Group UK Ltd.
UKHW021001140124
435975UK00009BA/289